Jesus in Back Alleys

Jesus in Back Alleys

The Story and Reflections of a Contemporary Prophet

Hubert Schwartzentruber

Foreword by Mary Lou Cummings

DreamSeeker Books
TELFORD, PENNSYLVANIA

an imprint of
Pandora Press U.S.

Copublished with
Herald Press
Scottdale, Pennsylvania

Pandora Press U.S. orders, information, reprint permissions:
pandoraus@netreach.net
1-215-723-9125
126 Klingerman Road, Telford PA 18969
www.PandoraPressUS.com

The paper used in this publication is recycled and meets the
minimum requirements of American National Standard for Information Sciences—Permanence of Paper for Printed Library Materials, ANSI Z39.48-1984.1984

All Bible quotations are used by permission, all rights reserved, and are from the *New Revised Standard Version Bible*, copyright 1989, by the Division of Christian Education of the
National Council of the Churches of Christ in the USA.

Library of Congress Cataloguing-in-Publication Data
Schwartzentruber, Huber, 1929-
    Jesus in back alleys: the story and reflections of a contemporary prophet /
    Hubert Schwartzentruber.
        p. cm.
    ISBN 1-931038-07-4 (pbk. : alk. paper)
        1. Schwartzentruber, Hubert, 1929- 2. Mennonites--United States--
    Clergy--Biography
    I. Title
BX8143.S37 A3 2002
289.7'092--dc21
[B]
                                                                2002026406

10 09 08 07 06 05 04 03 02   10 9 8 7 6 5 4 3 2 1

To my children:
Michael and his wife Diana and their children,
Johanna June and Jacob Edward;
Lorna and her husband Roberto and their son,
Umberto Maya.

Contents

Foreword

HUBERT SWARTZENTRUBER HAS SNOW-WHITE HAIR NOW; he has tried to retire three times. But somehow those of us who know him still regard him as a vigorous force, one still deeply engaged in the path of exploration and discovery.

Hubert's life seemed to intersect with many dramatic changes of the last fifty years: he grew up on a farm, speaking both German and English. But a call to ministry took him and his young wife June to spend formative marriage years in a St. Louis, Missouri, ghetto housing project. There they learned to love a new Jesus—one they met on the streets, at the funerals of gunshot and police brutality victims. They met Martin Luther King and learned from African-American community leaders. Still later, Hubert worked in Mennonite denominational offices, helping the church bridge culture gaps, teach peace in the face of the Vietnam War, and explore new forms of outreach.

After the death of his wife June, children Lorna and David now being adults, Hubert married Mary Rittenhouse, a former St. Louis volunteer, and moved to Pennsylvania. Here because of his gentle, courageous pastoral leadership, he was asked to chair a study group which might bring together various positions on homosexuality that had arisen in relation to Germantown Mennonite Church, for which Hubert was overseer. Once again, the man who should have been peacefully retired was embroiled in the middle of the culture's messiest controversy.

In these pages, Hubert tells us something about the internal path he walked as he moved from country to city, "religious" to secular, safety to danger. He gives a personal picture of the faith that sustained him and the Jesus who led him.

This memoir is not professional. It does not even attempt to be complete. Many stories with huge dramatic potential are surprisingly only hinted at. Rather, Hubert's recurring focus is his discovery of God's presence in the most humble and broken life and in the darkest corners. He takes great care to share with us Scriptures he has claimed as his own "mission statement," and which have fed his courage to step out into the uncharted territory where he believes Jesus is already walking.

Although he writes this small spiritual memoir on paper, Hubert wants to "carve in stone" one truth he has come to know: it is a sin to discriminate against any person created by God. The man who felt the heat from a KKK cross burning, heard bullets crash through his car window, and cried in public when his church voted not to include women as possible pastors, can still cry over injustice, prejudice, and religious apathy.

I had a sense as I read Hubert's words that he had prayed them as he wrote them. I felt privileged to read the testimony of the stories, Hubert's fervent hope that all he had learned about God's presence in the tough places would not be lost to us, who live in tough times. As he says, "We may never keep people guessing as to whose side we are on. Nor can we wait till we have all the answers before we can walk with . . . those who are oppressed. The answers come as we are walking."

This gentle pastor who loves John Deere tractors, polishes pieces of colorful stone as gifts, listens long and hard, writes love poems to his wife Mary—this man offers few pat answers to his friends and colleagues. He simply invites us to join the walk, in the company of Jesus and of the wounded ones in this world.

—*Mary Lou Cummings, Perkasie, Pennsylvania, is a teacher, congregational elder, and editor. She is author of* Surviving Without Romance: African Women Tell Their Stories.

Preface
and Acknowledgements

*I*N THIS VOLUME I REFLECT ON FORTY-FIVE YEARS as a minister seeking faithfully to preach the good news of peace. A variety of experiences shaped my understanding of what the good news is and what God is all about. My understanding of theology has been shaped by joys in ministry and by disappointments, by making mistakes and by making right choices. My ministry has been shaped by many people who have touched my life. It has been shaped by drinking deeply from the richness of other cultures. Above all it has been shaped by discovering truth in the Scriptures which throughout my life have been a beacon for me. I should note that although I have tried to learn from the biblical prophets, the subtitle of this book is not mine but was chosen by the publisher.

I am especially indebted to my two children, Michael and Lorna. Despite my spending so much time away from home "fixing" the world and the church when I should have been with them, I still sense their love for me.

My late wife June, mother of Michael and Lorna, was a special gift to many people. Her love for family and the church, as well as her caring concern for people who were forced by an unjust society to live on the margins, consumed her energy. Her voice for justice for oppressed people and for equal opportunity for women still speaks today. Without her love, compassion, wisdom, and commitment to justice—qualities she shared with me until her death—this book would never have become a reality.

My conclusions and responses to some issues that have consumed much of my energy are likely not ones some of my friends can accept. My chapter on homosexuality, for example, is a window into my pain over the fracture it has made in the church, which has caused alienation and fear. I have experienced deep peace in my own soul as I have wrestled with this issue. That peace is a buffer when the arrows from the bows of my critics fly at me.

I cannot name all the people who helped me write this book. I will name a few in addition to my children and my late wife June. I am indebted to Michael A. King and Pandora Press U.S./DreamSeeker Books for encouraging me to submit a manuscript. Michael's editorial gift has been like polish on stained silver.

I give credit to a very wise person is St. Louis, Missouri, Macler Shepard, a leader in the community whose wisdom I still seek. Macler's wisdom was sought by persons from all sectors of society, from President Carter to the homeless on the street. The Bethesda Mennonite Church people in St. Louis accepted me and nurtured me. The many persons who spent some time in St. Louis in voluntary service all contributed to bring clarity as to what the church is all about in the world. Cecil and Judy Miller, whose spirit lingered in St. Louis after they moved away, continue to share their caring concerns and wisdom with the community. I also left a major part of myself in St. Louis. I have recurring dreams of being engaged in some activity with Macler Shepard.

During our years in Elkhart, Indiana, it was friends like Dale and Laura Schumm, John and Shirley Powell, Hubert and Helen Brown, Willard and Alice Roth, and members of Southside Fellowship, to name only a few, whose friendship we highly valued. I had occasion during those years to be a guest speaker at many congregations throughout the Mennonite constituency. In every congregation a core of people deeply committed to peace and justice gave me courage to preach the good news of peace. The staff at Board of Congregational Ministries, of which I was a part, helped me to broaden my vision of peacemaking.

The team of people who served on the missions committee for the Mennonite Conference of Eastern Canada became a special gift to me. I felt their support when I attempted to give leadership in developing new congregations with a goal that every congregation become a special gift from God to its community. The leaders of the conference modeled for me what the good news of peace is all about.

My close association with Herb Schultz during those days was a rich blessing. We could laugh, cry, and pray together on some of our long trips to visit congregations. I should name many more persons who enriched my life during those years. I would be amiss if I did not give credit to Ralph Lebold, whose wisdom I sought out and respected.

The Danforth Mennonite Church in Toronto provided us with a community of friends. Even though we are away from Toronto for more than a decade it still feels like home when we go back to visit. In eastern Pennsylvania the congregations I served as overseer helped me to grow in my understanding of what the gospel is all about. The friendships we formed at Spring Mount Mennonite Church, where I was pastor for five years, remain a special treasure. It is at Plains Mennonite Church, where we are currently members and I served for two years as interim pastor, that we receive day-to-day spiritual nurture and friendship.

I did not write much about my present ministry as chaplain at Souderton Mennonite Homes. The staff and residents there continue to teach me about peace and justice. Ministering to and being ministered by people who are in the homestretch of life is another significant window into God's gracious gift of life.

It is from the most unlikely people that my greatest source of encouragement has come. Many times it has come from the people whom society had long rejected and forgotten. For them, and for all our friends scattered across the country, we are thankful.

Without the support, encouragement, and love I receive from my wife, Mary Rittenhouse, the joy of ministry would have faded away. Mary's caring spirit and compassion models what I have tried to preach. Her actions are sermons of love and justice. I often feel tears of joy trickling down my cheek when she sings solos in church. I thank God over and over for the blessing she has been to me.

If I were to write this book a year from now, I likely would have to add some new insight I have not had before. My experience of the past rooted the themes of peace and justice deeply into my understanding of the Scriptures and faithfulness in discipleship. Whether now or later, I say with Paul, "I press on toward the goal for the prize of the heavenly call of God in Christ Jesus" (Phil. 3:14).

—*Hubert Schwartzentruber*
Telford, Pennsylvania

Jesus in Back Alleys

Chapter 1

From Lake Huron to June's Grave and Beyond

OVER THE DRY SINK IN OUR KITCHEN IN Toronto, Ontario, hung a painting framed in a window of the old barn from the farm in Huron County, the place of my birth. The farm served as a university for me in my growing-up days. I learned something about agriculture. To be a farmer you had to be somewhat of a mechanic. There was business training on the farm. To work with animals you had to have some veterinary knowledge. You needed to operate machinery. It was important to have weather forecasting ability.

It was on the farm that I learned to respect the very precious gift of fertile soil God has given to us. Soil is the womb of life. It nurtures tiny seeds that grow into trees and produce fruit to sustain life.

It was on the farm that I learned about love, love from my parents, love from my siblings and extended family, love felt in the Zurich Mennonite Church were I made my commitment to Christ and was baptized and licensed for ministry.

The fall clouds that hung over beautiful Lake Huron taught me to look up and marvel at the beauty of God's creation. I enjoyed gazing at the formation of the clouds. In my imagination I saw many mind-stretching images as though an artist with a long handled brush painted her most creative feelings on a canvas in the sky.

On that farm on the Goshen Line, five kilometers south of Zurich, Ontario, I learned to speak two languages before I was six. I learned how to plant a garden. A favorite task of mine was to drive the team of horses. I still recall how proud I was one evening when I brought the team to the barn and announced that I had plowed two acres that day. Steering the one furrow walking plow with two spirited horses, lines around my back, and occasionally being heaved into the air when the plow hit a rock, was more than recreation.

I always had a problem with making the horses work so hard. Sometimes the horses developed sore shoulders from the collars around their necks. I felt some of the pain they must have felt. I made frequent stops to give the horses their much-deserved rest. I even sneaked a few extra oats for them at dinner time.

I can't begin to describe how happy I was when we got our first John Deere tractor. I have fond memories of taking the last team of horses to the fifty-acre pasture field and there turning them loose to enjoy the lush grass and to frolic in the summer sun.

I was pleased we were spared milking cows. Beef cattle were our major livestock. Shorthorn cattle were my favorite. I still wonder why I did not protest when the calves that grew up into graceful animals were sent off to the slaughterhouse.

Despite the many hog pens I cleaned, I did not develop the same affection for hogs. I always had a voluminous appetite for bacon, cured ham and pork sausage. I would likely still line a plate with sausage for breakfast were it not for my good wife Mary, who has so much better judgment regarding healthy food. She tells me she does not want to get to heaven and have to account for my life being shortened due to eating sausage. My response is that she may have to give an account for making me wait so long to get there.

I always looked forward to spring when the baby chicks arrived. The brooder house stove was stoked with coal. Fresh straw or wood shaving on the floor greeted the fluffy little balls that trustingly huddled by the warmth of the fire. If I ever had any doubts about God, they disappeared when I watched the contented little chicks.

My brothers loved to hunt. I never developed a craving for guns and bullets. I did try hunting a few times but could never bring myself to take the life of a rabbit whom I supposed its mother had given a name. I enjoyed the deer in the wild too much to kill them. And so inevitably my hunting career was short-lived.

I have memories of the two-kilometer walk on cold wintry mornings to the old one-room country school called the Tin School. The old rail fences along the side of the road provided a resting-place for the snow drifting across the open plowed fields. The top of the snow banks often reached to the wires on the telephone lines. It was fun climbing those drifts and sliding down the other side. When the weather was really bad, our school bus was a team of horses and a sled. Riding on the hay on the sled, with sleigh bells ringing on the horses, was always a special treat.

When the days got longer in late February, we often went outside after the evening meal to play in the snowdrifts. We would dig caves or make tunnel through the drifts between the house and the barn. A six-foot drift was not unusual after a blustery winter storm.

There was no TV to be glued to during the long stormy winter evenings. But there were neighbors to visit. Many an evening was spent at Harold and Beatrice's house playing cards around the kitchen table.

The cold wind blowing against the window was not equal to the warmth of the old wood stove. While the gales howled through the leafless trees we exchanged stories, ate popcorn, and drank cider.

Spring was always an exciting time on the farm. While the snow was melting the tractor and implements were being prepared to cultivate the soil, plant the seed, and expect a harvest in the fall. I recall turning the crank on the old fanning mill as the seed grain was cleaned and prepared for the spring seeding. Day by day we watched the snow disappear and the dry ground call for the cultivator and the drill to plant the precious seed. Spring was a time of renewal of spirit after the long cold and dark days of winter.

I do not remember any year harvest failed to come. There was something special about getting the binder out when the wheat turned a golden brown. The old John Deere showed off its green and yellow, parading its glory pulling the binder through the lush wheat field. Sheaf after sheaf was turned out, and the sheaf carrier dropped them into neat rows.

After the binder made its last round and the rabbits ran out from their hiding place, the hard work began. Every sheaf was placed into a shock to dry in the sun and await the day for the thresher to come.

On threshing day the community all worked together to help each other do the harvest. I could still make myself believe I can hear George coming down the road with the old Rumley tractor pulling the big machine. Soon several farmers appeared with horses and wagons while others came to pitch the sheaves onto the wagons. Load after load was hauled to the hungry threshing machine as the old Rumley snorted long puffs of smoke into the air until the fields were empty.

My task usually was to drive the team of horses and level the loads as two men pitched the sheaves onto the wagon. Sometimes the wagon would jerk so hard I would land face first in a bed of thistles that grew along with the wheat.

The drive with a big load of sheaves to the machine was always reinforced with a little prayer that the load would not fall apart before we got there. One by one we pitched each sheaf into the hungry feeder. The hot summer wind seemed to delight in blowing dust and straw back to coat our sweaty bodies.

I always had a morbid fear of snakes. On occasions when the wagon was unloaded there was a little snake slithering on the wagon bed. But snakes and dust and thistles were soon forgotten when everyone sat down to enjoy a threshers' meal. There seemed to be no limit to how much roast beef, mashed potatoes, and gravy one could eat. The meal was always topped off with a big piece of pie.

My parents, like many others who came through the Great Depression, could not afford to drive an automobile. Horse and buggy were our method of transportation during those years.

In the five-kilometers drive to town there was opportunity to see the flowers that were growing alongside of the road. One could even see a mouse run for a hiding place from the eyes of the hawk that was circling in the sky above looking for a fresh meal. There was time to stop to talk to the neighbor who was mending the fence along the road. The pace was slow enough to see the beauty in stones as well as the color of the leaves and to smell the new-mown hay.

The speed at which we travel now leaves no room to enjoy the beauty along the way, much less to chat with neighbors and friends. Friendship is the glue that keeps a society healthy. Once we no longer have time to cultivate friendships our values in society begin to crumble.

One of the early memories I have of my mother was the suffering she endured with gallstone attacks. One of the last memories I have of her, when I was eight years old, was being in her room at the hospital the evening before she died. I know exactly where I was playing the next day when I was told she had died. Even though I was eight, I otherwise have limited memory of her.

I have faint memories of Mother's funeral. Her body was not taken to a funeral home. Embalming took place at home.

On the day of the funeral many people gathered at the house. There was a brief service there then a long procession of cars went to the church. Another longer service took place at the church.

The church service was followed by another procession to the cemetery. At the cemetery there was another short service. I do remember one song that was sung at the grave side. It had a line, "We are going down the valley one by one, with our faces toward the setting of the sun."

We as a family hardly ever talked about our mother. Unfortunately emotions were seldom expressed in those days.

I recall playing with friends some weeks after her death when one wished to comfort me by saying, "Your mother will soon be back." But already at age eight I knew she would not be back. I wonder even today what it would have been like to grow up with a mother.

But then I *did* grow up with a mother. My father was both a mother and a father to me. I had many mothers: aunts who cared for me, friends who showed love and kindness, neighbors who were like extended families.

A cousin of mine, closer to the age of my parents, requested that I join their family. My father's good judgment was that I stay with him. The family of the cousin who offered to take me were like parents to me as long as they lived. In a letter from them after I began ministry in the inner city they said, "There isn't a day that we do not pray for you."

My father actively attended church and lived his faith in daily practice. As an early teen I did not care to go to church any more. I was permitted to make my decision not to go but was always encouraged to go. Out of respect for my father, I always went to the spring and fall revival meetings. I look back now at those meetings with mixed emotions. I lay awake many a night afraid that the Rapture might take place and I would be left all alone. I would listen for sounds to hear if the rest of the household was still there.

Hell as described by the evangelists certainly was not the place I wanted to go to. I remember the charts the evangelists had in front of the church. The charts showed the history of how God moved in the past and outlined the events yet to come. What they described as what was yet to come was not pleasant at all. To question anything the evangelist said would surely bring punishment from God. I recall hell being described in such dramatic ways that one could almost smell the brimstone and feel the heat of the fire. As for the chart, it seemed to me God only had to look at the chart to see what to do next.

The invitation to escape hell and go to heaven was always a long, drawn-out affair. The evangelist would say, "We'll sing one last verse." That final verse was usually the first of many more. Those were quiet moments. A few eyes were looking around to see who was going to stand or raise their hands. Others were in deep prayer. Some were watching the clock. Others were patiently waiting for the last amen.

I look back at those experiences and wonder if there would not have been a better way to invite people to place their faith in Christ and receive forgiveness for sin. I may not criticize that generation, because they presented the gospel as sincerely as they knew how. Yet being sincere must always be integrated with a deep search for truth. Our inviting of others to faith should always be presented out of compassion, not fear. But God was always presented to me as a very angry Being. I perceived God standing over me with a club ready to strike me down the moment I made a wrong move. I was never sure I could make any moves good enough for God to honor.

The God I knew was limited to the Mennonite church. My Catholic, Lutheran, and evangelical friends would never make it to heaven. Years later, while visiting my brother who lived close to the Catholic cemetery, I took a little stroll among the tombstones. There were the names of the parents of my closest friends. I remembered their lives and their love. While reading those names, I sensed a peace and expectation within me that they, along with my Mennonite family, would greet me when I arrived in God's precious presence.

But it was in that Mennonite church on the north end of Zurich that I found faith. It was during one of those revival meetings, which I now see from another point of view, that I made my decision to commit my life to Christ. It was not the preaching that convicted me. It was not the tear-jerking songs that moved me. It wasn't even the belabored invitation. It was the friends I sensed cared about me.

One person was a bright light to me in my search for meaning to fill my life. Albert Martin never preached to me. He went out of his way to befriend me. His life was a model of what a disciple of Jesus should be. His expressions were of joy and peace. I decided if being a Christian produced that kind of a life, I wanted to share in it too.

There were leaders in the congregation whose lives were not always an example of the Spirit of Christ. They could speak the proper pious language on Sunday but conveniently lay it down on Monday. But Albert's testimony was so strong that the negative testimony of others could not blind me to the Spirit's tender gentle call to faith.

A few years later Albert became the pastor of my church. I had the privilege to serve in various capacities of leadership in the congregation. A call came to the congregation to ordain a deacon. The bishops came to discern the voice of the congregation and proceed to select the person for the office. My name with six other persons was suggested. I was perhaps nineteen. I sensed a call to ministry. In my youthful enthusiasm, I thought likely this was the time God was calling and setting me aside for this specific task.

The bishops visited with each of the candidates. In my interview, I do not remember being asked anything about my faith. They did ask if I had life insurance and if I did, would I be willing to surrender it. Of course a nineteen-year-old Mennonite boy in rural Ontario fifty years ago was not a prime candidate to have a life insurance policy. I also had to promise I would marry a good wife. That promise I kept.

The Sunday afternoon for the ordination service came. The selection processes was helped by use of the lot. Seven books were placed on a table in front of us. One book had in it a slip indicating that whoever chose this book was the person God had called. We each selected our book and quietly proceeded back to our seats.

I was the last in the row of the seven candidates. The drama began when the bishop stepped down from the pulpit and began the process of opening book by book to find the lot. There was painful silence in the crowded church. Ordination services had an appeal to infrequent church participants. Sometimes I wonder if, on the sly, some betting was going on.

The bishop opened the first book and the lot was not there. As he proceeded down the line my heart beat faster. One by one the holders of the books were excluded from the call. The final moment came when the person next to me handed his book to the bishop. If the lot was not there it had to be in my book. The lot was in his book.

I can't begin to describe the feeling that arose inside me. It was a feeling of both rejection and relief. Was my sense of call for ministry wrong? As I look back now, it would have been a disaster had the lot fallen on me. In the few years following, the congregation ground up several pastors. The person ordained as deacon led a group of followers out of the church to form a conservative group. I believe now that my not being selected was God's love and grace protecting me from a situation that could have destroyed me.

While there was pain and conflict and division in the congregation in Zurich, there were also many things that were right. I am not sure I could repeat the title of any sermon I heard from the pulpit during all my years in that congregation. But I have many good memories of being nurtured in silent ways by people who had the capacity to preach without words.

I have distinct memory of the first pastor of my childhood days. His name was Christian Schrag. I do not remember his preaching but do remember how he always took time to shake hands with little children. He made me feel as though I was a person too.

My first adventure away from home was to attend the Ontario Mennonite Bible School. I was shy and unprepared for any serious study. I can't think of many in our congregation who attended high school during my growing up days. But my sense of call to ministry prompted me to move forward.

I reflected earlier that our congregation fed us a heavy dose of premillenialism. A teacher, John Garber, did not accept the millenialist position. He was forbidden by the Bible school board to teach any other view. On several occasions he would take a few of us off campus and share with us his understanding of what the kingdom of Jesus Christ was all about. This freed me to experience God as a God of grace and not a God with a club. My sleepless nights for fear of the Rapture taking place were over.

After five terms at the Bible school and Bible institute, I faced whether to go on to college. Not having had high school, I needed to take GED tests. I used the passing of those tests as a fleece to determine if I should go on to college. I passed the test and said good-bye to the farm I loved so much and made my journey to Eastern Mennonite College (now Eastern Mennonite University, in Harrisonburg, Virginia).

I remember the loneliness I experienced at EMU on the day my father had an auction to sell the farm implements and livestock. I would no longer care for the cows I saw growing up from little calves. The John Deere tractor was gone. I was away at college and would never see those animals again. Despite the pain inside of me I also had a sense of peace. My love for the farm was superceded by my call to ministry. There were, however, times of disappointment in ministry when I wondered if I should not have stayed on the farm.

Without proper foundation of math or science, I struggled away in college until graduation. My grades kept me humble. While my professors and teachers did not tell me everything I needed to know to make life choices, they provided a foundation on which to build my faith.

It was at college that I made good the promise I made to the bishop when I went through the lot for deacon. I promised I would marry a good wife. June Lambke soon caught my eye. On our first date we went for a hike with some friends to the mountain. We hiked unaware that the sun was disappearing. To find our way back, we needed to follow each other very closely, stay in good communication, and observe carefully the curves and rocks in our path.

That was a journey that lasted twenty-seven years. There were rocks and curves in our path. Darkness did set in at times. June enjoyed life but never good health. She cherished life until summer 1984, when finally the heart that had given her problems since birth no longer supplied the energy she needed. The memories of June's deep longing for justice for all, her agony over discrimination against women in leadership, her concern for equality of all people, and her gently caring personality are treasured by family and the many friends who loved her.

June had her funeral arrangements filed with a funeral director. The directions called for no embalming of the body. She selected a very plain casket with no frills. The cost of the funeral was a fraction of what it would have been for a regular funeral. The money a normal funeral would have cost was set aside for a scholarship fund especially for women who wanted to prepare for pastoral ministry or leadership in the area of peace and justice.

It was not easy to follow June's wishes for the funeral arrangements. The question, What will people think, nagged at us. But when I read now, some fifteen years later, that people are still benefitting from the fund, I know we did the right thing. I can imagine that when a candidate receives some of that money, June sends a smile and blessing to them. Perhaps she sends also an intercession that the candidate be given the grace and freedom to proclaim boldly, like the prophets of old, that justice be done for all. June's physical pain often was hidden. But she could not hide the pain she experienced when women who sensed a call to pastoral ministry were denied ordination because of gender.

Like all good parents we were proud of our two children, Michael and Lorna. I look back now and regret that I did not spend more time with my family. My work as pastor in the inner city took much of my time, and I will talk more about that later. I also served on a variety of churchwide boards and committees, which frequently took me away from home. I never seemed to learn to say no when invited to speak at meetings and conferences. I learned much too late to put my family first. I have heard many similar stories from other pastors and church employees. I am thankful, then, for the love I continually receive from my children.

I recall one of my history professors said one time, "We tend to see history not as history is but as we are." It likely is true that we interpret Scriptures much the same way. Who I am and my life experiences are reflected in my understanding of God at work among his people.

I'm not sure I always arrived at the right answers, but they were answers for me at the moment. The decisions I made may not always have been the best ones, yet I look back at many decisions that time has now confirmed for me were the right ones. Some were life-changing for me. I suppose some decision-making was fueled by degrees of anger, but tempered with joy and peace.

The most important events in my life were the ones that taught me more about the "Word becoming flesh and dwelling with human beings." In the next few chapters I will tell some stories of my ministry that shaped my understanding of the gospel, the good news of peace through Jesus Christ, found so often less on Main Street than in a society's back alleys.

Chapter 2

Preaching While They Scream Outside: God Calls a Good News People

ON A WALL IN MY OFFICE HANGS A SKETCH of the Pruitt Igoe Housing Project in St. Louis, Missouri. An art teacher who was in voluntary service presented us with one of her paintings when she returned home after a summer in the city. For some thirty years it has served to remind me of some of the lessons God taught me while ministering in the inner city. Some of the lesson I learned were lessons my seminary professors could not teach me.

It was a late fall afternoon when my wife June and I, married only six weeks, arrived in St. Louis. We responded to an invitation of Mennonite Board of Missions to develop a new congregation in St. Louis, Missouri. The area chosen for us to work in was the city's Near North Side in the Pruitt Igoe Housing Project.

Pruitt Igoe was made up of about forty 11-story buildings on a fifty-acre site with housing for 15 thousand low-income people. Every apartment in the brick buildings had concrete floors. The elevators stopped only every other floor. We lived on ninth and the elevator stopped at eighth and tenth. We always needed to walk either up one floor or down one.

The narrow little dark stairways were also the scene of drug pushing and all sorts of other activity. Often lights were broken and people had to feel their way, hoping not be accosted. The elevators often served as bathrooms, which made them unattractive while riding ten floors hoping not to experience an elevator breakdown between forth and fifth floors.

I'm not sure that all the apartments in the project were ever fully occupied. Pruitt Igoe was branded as the number one crime area in the city. It got national attention for its failure to provide safe, affordable housing. When a crime was committed in the North Side, it was always associated with Pruitt Igoe. A church leader friend visited us one time. At 3:45 in the afternoon, about five thousand children burst out of the four schools in the area into the streets. "My, it must take a missionary spirit to live here!" he exclaimed.

James and Rowena Lark, then retired, had been asked to go to St. Louis for several months to do ground work to establish the first Mennonite church in that area. James Lark was the first African-American bishop in the Mennonite church. His vision for missions was at least one, if not two, generations ahead of the rest of the church. Back in the 1940s he already had a jump-start on the church growth movement of the 1980s and 1990s.

The Larks' vision was rooted deeply in their culture and faith. I often wonder how our Mennonite mission emphasis would be structured today if the mission leaders of that day had had the foresight to allow the Larks' insights to shape Mennonite church visions. The highly motivated and deeply committed people directing missions did not all have the opportunity to drink deeply from another culture. Early urban missions were developed through the eyes of traditional Mennonite Germanic understanding of the world. And that world often was rather small.

I am not casting stones on the faithful work of the saints of the past. I simply want to recognize the culture and times of an era. James and Rowena Lark had a special ability with potential to open doors to new understandings and approaches for carrying out the mission of the church. The Larks' vision and gifts in developing new congregations were an inspiration to June and me as we naively approached building a new congregation in the inner city. Too soon after we arrived, however, the Larks went back into retirement again.

June had worked for a number of years as a secretary in the home missions office of Mennonite Board of Missions in Elkhart, Indiana. She had much more insight than I into what was involved in venturing out into a new community to develop a new congregation. June had gifts to be much more than a secretary and to do the bidding of another person (valid though that can be). But because she was a female, she was not given a direct leadership role. Could she have used the good gifts God gave her already in her youth, I think the mission strategy of the church would have moved at least one generation beyond where it was then.

I'm thankful that today women can play important roles in church leadership, such as presidents of colleges, moderators of denominational bodies, and pastors of congregations. Likely today June could be president of the board instead of a secretary. That is not devalue the role of a secretary. Secretaries play an important role in any institution. Often the secretaries shape the program and provide the insight for the executive director. What is bad is for the person who knows more about the program than the director not to be allowed in the director role because of gender.

June also grew up on a farm near the town of Preston, now Cambridge, Ontario, the oldest of four children. Her parents were active church members. She worked as a secretary for a few years in a potato chip factory, but her call to mission led her to go into voluntary service and then to be on staff at Mennonite Board of Missions (MBM). After a number of years she decided to go on to college, where we met each other.

After we were engaged, I had a conversation with the MBM executive director. I told him of my relationship with June. His response was, "She is a jewel." Even though her health limited her somewhat in physical activity, it never prevented her from serving and caring about other people. When I was licensed for ministry, the bishop in charge also blessed June as a deaconess. Her commissioning was never recorded because it would not have been been considered appropriate at that time to give such a charge to a women. In reality June functioned as a pastor, teacher, counselor, and bishop. But she never had the title.

She did, however, have the title of trusted friend. The highest honor Jesus ever bestowed on anyone was to call them a friend. Like Abraham, June was a friend of God.

We both had all the credentials needed for inner-city church development. We were newly married, never lived in a city, had farm experience in rural Ontario, did not know any person on a first-name basis who was not of European descent. Best of all, we were fresh out of college so still had all our answers intact.

While I had all the answers, I did not know what most of the questions were. I still don't know what all the questions are, but I know many more than I did then. Answers must be found in the context where the questions are asked. I have also learned that some of the easy answers to complex questions are not the right ones. Many people have lost faith in the church and in God because the church is prone to give answers without making any attempt to know what the questions are.

The questions become clearer when we live among the people with whom we are struggling to find answers. A good answer today might not be a good answer tomorrow because the context in which we search for answers changes. Some answers that fit well in my rural home community did not make much sense in the inner city where life is lived a day at a time.

The creation story suggests that out of chaos God created order. For a farm boy with Amish roots, fresh out of college and newly married, the inner city seemed like chaos. But what I viewed as disorder was also a new fresh, orderly context for me to hear the Scriptures speak. Out of what I viewed as chaos God started a process in me to bring order into my understanding of the gospel.

Classrooms, libraries, and study halls are important to developing our theology. The writings of the great minds over the centuries have valuable instruction for today. The acts of God in history as recorded in the Scriptures give courage and reassurance that God still speaks to and guides the people of the kingdom. Professors who have studied and worked hard and prayed for wisdom to share with their students are a special gift from God.

Meanwhile theology that is tested in the streets and back alleys, scrutinized by the marginalized, exposed to a fragmented society, questioned by the skeptic, and tried in the court of the oppressed is a theology that is trustworthy. The classroom and the street must be equal partners in theological reflection.

I am thankful for my classroom teachers. They gave me a solid foundation I could take into the street to be tested. From insight and knowledge gained from studies in the classroom I could make responses as I was confronted in the street. I also had teachers in the street. They were the gang members, wineheads, angry civil rights leaders, mothers crushed by unjust welfare systems. The wise people who could see through the political system all helped me to interpret the theology I learned in the classroom. They helped me clarify some of the questions I thought I knew and had answers for.

The day we moved into a ninth-floor apartment in the Pruitt Igoe Housing Project was also the day we needed to learn to listen in a new way. We needed to listen to the six hundred other people who shared the one apartment building with us. We were interested in staying physically alive amid a community trained in violence. To stay alive we needed to make friends quickly with those with whom we shared the same elevator. And we had to make friends on their terms and not ours. They did not invite us to come. We invaded their territory. It became important for us to work toward trust relationships so we would receive an invitation from the community to stay.

The community did not need us as much as we needed them. We did not have the luxury of choosing our friends but needed to accept the offers of friendship that came to us. As I look back now, had we not taken the opportunity to make friends with our neighbors on their terms we likely would not have survived the turbulent sixties.

After cultivating friendships, eating at each other's tables, going for rides together in the country, telling each other our stories, we were invited to stay. After fifteen years it was a painful experience to tell the congregation that emerged during those years that we were accepting a call to a position in our denominational office.

I look back now and wonder at times if we made the right decision to leave. In my memory I will always hear Alice crying when she heard we were leaving. Alice was disabled because of breaking her hip when she was a child. She never received care from a doctor. She was placed on a bed between two boards to keep her hip together. Her walking was always limited to crutches. We were able to minister to her, but she really ministered more to us. There were few days she did not pray for us. Prayer is an ingredient that can be overlooked when one gets deeply involved in ministry. When Alice died some time after we left, she requested that her meager savings be divided between our children and the children of another family.

Coming fresh out of college, I was eager to expound all the theology I knew. I assumed faithfulness to the gospel was to speak the right words and encourage people to believe the right doctrine. The right doctrine for me was the belief that was shaped by my culture. I loved my pulpit. The pulpit is one of the safest places to be when you are not sure of yourself. If you don't have the guts to confront a person face-to-face, you can scream at them from behind the pulpit. If you have within yourself a streak of ambition to become an actor, you can always practice from behind the pulpit. If you're not sure what you are saying, you can raise your voice to a high pitch. If you have a hobby or pet subject you want to nurture, you can use pulpit time for that.

No one ever held a gun to my face when I was behind the pulpit. But they did in the street. No one ever beat me to unconsciousness while in the pulpit but they did in the street. Without my knowing it, those thoughts might have been present in the pews when I preached. Especially when I talked about following Jesus in daily life being more acceptable to God than affirming a right belief.

Please let me quickly say that ministry from the pulpit is of utmost importance. But the preachers of the gospel speak empty words from the pulpit until they have practiced their theology in the street. The pulpit and street ministries must be joined; let no one devise a sword sharp enough to divide the two.

I preached many sermons at the little church at 2823 Dayton Street. A broken pane in a stained glass window at the rear of the church was replaced with a clear glass. I could look out through that little window while I was preaching. Sometimes I could see gang members gathering at the most notable drug distribution place in the neighborhood. I could see mothers with three or four toddlers make their way to the corner store to get some food for breakfast.

I still remember a fight I witnessed one time when I looked out the window while preparing a sermon. Someone dragged another man by his legs down fourteen stairs. He then stood over him with an axe, ready to split his head wide open. A scene like that gives you a certain inspiration you did not get in a homiletics class. The noise of sirens, screams, and cursing one could hear from outside were often louder than the "Amens" from the pews. It was not long until I started to ask myself, How does what I preach from the pulpit relate to what goes on out in the street?

I liked the pulpit because it was "safe" and my tailor-made answers fit. The streets were "dangerous" and the answers had to be sought out of the questions being asked there. It can be a painful process to make shifts in our thinking and beliefs. Because of some violent acts in the community, my theology underwent some testing. I'm sure my theological understanding is still in process, still bearing the marks of that testing. Once we have finally crystalized our thinking, then perhaps we are looking toward entering the dementia unit in the retirement home.

There had been a series of police shootings in a six-block area surrounding the church. The first funeral I ever officiated at was for a young man shot by the police. The father of the man told me the story of his death.

The young man was a suspect in a store break-in. He was spotted in the alley and the police called for him to stop. The young men in the street were afraid of the police, knowing that if they were arrested they would be taken to the police station and beaten within an inch of their life until they confessed to the crime, whether they had committed it or not. This young man was familiar with those stories and wanted to avoid the beating, so he kept running. While he was running, the police shot him in the leg. While he lay wounded in the alley, I was told, the police pumped three more bullets into his head.

I remember another story of an arrest of a young man that happened about the same time. This young man was arrested, searched, and handcuffed, put in the back seat of the police cruiser, and taken to the police station. While in the cruiser with his hands cuffed, he was shot and killed by the police. The story in the paper said the police shot the young man in self-defense.

I was informed that the young man had a story to tell that would have embarrassed the police. I don't know what information that young man had. But I failed to see that being handcuffed and seated in the back of a cruiser without any weapons made him a threat to any one, regardless of the reasons for his arrest.

Several other senseless killings by police had taken place in our community within a few weeks. A community group decided they needed to put forth some effort to address this senseless waste of human lives. A few people visited police headquarters. They wanted to converse with the chief of police in hopes of developing better understanding between police and the community. When they arrived, they were told no one would see them. They repeated the visit again the next day but received the same response.

The community group decided to invite as many people as would go to march with them in large numbers to police headquarters. I was working in the church that morning, getting ready for "pulpit" ministry, when Macler Shepard visited me. We had a friendly conversation. Macler then told me the march was planned for that afternoon and asked if I would participate. All of a sudden my pulpit felt so safe. I did not want to march in the street. In fact, I even thought it wrong to participate in protest marches. The work of the pastor was to preach the gospel. What did marching with tired, weary people have to do with preaching the gospel?

I quickly had to make a decision. *If I don't go*, I argued with myself, *then I am giving a message that I am on the side of the oppressor. If I go I am identifying myself with the oppressed. But if I go*, I further reasoned, *some people there may not be Christians. There may be communists in the crowd.* I grew up having been taught that we must not to be unequally yoked with unbelievers. But a word seemed to come to me, *You must show whose side you are on.*

I said to Macler, "I will be there to march with you at one o'clock." It was the only right thing for me to do. I needed to listen to the voice of the community in which I lived, prayed, and worked. My assignment was to build a congregation in that community. A congregation that does not reflect the voice of the community is at best a body struggling for survival and at worst an enemy of the truth.

I put on my clergy collar and joined about 300 others in the march that afternoon. I wore a clergy collar when I was out in the street. After I was once attacked by three armed robbers, the police advised me to identify myself as a minister when I was out in the neighborhood. I suppose that even thugs know that ministers are so poorly paid robbing them is a waste of time.

On the march that day, I got the greatest compliment I ever received. As I marched with the people down Franklin Avenue, we came to a corner tavern. At the door of the tavern stood a big burly bartender. When I got to within ten feet of him, he spotted my collar. I heard him call out to the people at the bar, "Come and see the stupid preacher marching with them today." I shall always treasure that compliment. My identity was clear. Even the bartender knew whose side I was on. I never did go back to thank him for the compliment.

A mistaken identity is too great a price for kingdom people to pay. We may never keep people guessing as to whose side we are on. Nor can we wait till we have all the answers before we can walk with and stand beside those who are oppressed. The answers come as we are walking.

Jesus always stood with those who needed healing and those who had not yet experienced the *shalom* of God. Jesus often offended the religious community when he identified himself with the marginal and outcasts of society. He did not only offend them, he drove them into a rage so that they sought ways to justify killing him. They finally accomplished the murderous act they harbored in their heart.

Working for justice often receives its greatest opposition from the religious community. Whenever the answers of the community do not fit the questions of the oppressed, the community goes on the defensive. Their Main Street "answers" seem to them more important than the people suffering because of wrong answers. The religious community by its very nature is forced to oppose those who, from life's back alleys, try to bring in healing and hope in ways not yet approved by the institution. The reality of pain and suffering inflicted on people by an unjust society can easily be shelved in the process of discerning truth and making truth conform to the institution. Yet ultimately truth must conform to the bringing of healing and hope as Jesus brought. Institutions threatened by the truth of the gospel have lost their identity.

An apostate church is not a church that has ceased believing in the Scriptures. Nor is it a church that denies the resurrection, problematic though these moves may be. An apostate church may strongly affirm life after death. It may hold revival meetings and carefully search the Scriptures to understand right doctrine.

What makes a church apostate is that it no longer cares for the poor and the oppressed. It no longer hears the voices of the homeless in the street. It cannot hear the cries of the unwed mothers. It cannot see through the fog of the unjust political systems. It cannot feel the hopelessness of surviving on welfare. It cannot feel the pain of the people with AIDS. It cannot understand the violence committed by other Christians toward persons created with same-sex attraction. An apostate church supports politicians who make laws that favor the wealthy and take from the poor. The Scriptures caution over making judgment, but the apostate church readily judges those it does not understand. "Not all who say Lord, Lord will enter the kingdom of heaven," the Scripture says.

When the institution is threatened, it finds ways to condemn all people whose life experiences are different from its own. It can justify discrimination by use of Scripture and stand idly by when people are victimized because of how they were created by the Creator. Slavery in America, for instance, could not have lasted as long as it did were it not for the sermons preached on Sunday in support of slavery.

Let me return to the march on police headquarters. The marchers had planned to stay at headquarters until someone was willing to talk to them. I was prepared to sleep on the cold concrete steps until dialogue took place. I knew June would bring me a sandwich and a blanket as night set in. When the police saw the crowd, the chief became available to talk. It was the beginning of continuing conversation and cooperation with the police. It resulted in the police opening a storefront community relations office. They made a bus available to the community for special outings for children and adults. They often consulted with the community as they planned program.

The newly opened Community Police Relations office made a significant difference in the community. I recall Officer Thomas from Police Relations stopping by my office before Christmas. He inquired if I knew of some person who would serve as Santa Clause for distribution of candy to neighborhood children. The plan was to bring in Santa by helicopter, land on the street, and out would pop Santa with a big bag of goodies. Of course I knew who would be the right person to invite. I suggested Gene Gentry, a loyal member of the church and respected in the community.

As we were talking, Gene happened to came by. We asked him to volunteer for this little task. Gene consented, and by eleven o'clock that morning he was ready to board the helicopter. He was decked in his Santa suit with a huge bag of candy. What I did not know was that Gene was petrified to fly in a helicopter. But he kept that little secret. With much fear he entered the helicopter.

The word went out in the community that Santa was coming. The crowd of children was much like the crowd that surrounded Jesus when he made bread. There wasn't enough to go around. Jesus could make more bread, but Gene could not make more candy.

When Gene got out of the helicopter, the children swarmed toward him and took the candy. Gene hurried back in the helicopter in fear of his life. Later Gene and I could laugh over that incident, but at the moment Gene had second thoughts about ever trusting me again.

A group of people met that evening after the march to talk about the events of the day. I felt for the first time that all the doors in the community were open for me. I had identified myself. The community knew with whom I identified. I felt that I had gained the trust and respect of the community. Had I refused to identify with the hurting community the doors would have remained closed. The bullets that went by my head likely would have gone through my head. The goal of the organizers of the march was to bring about communication and reconciliation between the police department and the community. I would not have survived the ferment of the 60s had I not put forth effort to walk with and learn from the community that I sensed God called me to minister to.

Jesus identified with the poor and the outcasts. When the accusers of a prostitute wanted Jesus' support to carry out the death sentence he defended her. Perhaps the very people who had committed adultery with her were in the circle of the accusers. Jesus wrote something in the sand. Perhaps he wrote the names of those standing around her who had committed adultery with her. He then invited those who were without sin to cast the first stone and begin the execution process. One by one they started to walk away until all were gone. As she stood alone with Jesus he spoke words of forgiveness to her.

Jesus said that it is sin to refuse to stand with the oppressed. We are to care for the needy and welcome strangers.

"Come, you who are blessed by my Father, inherit the kingdom prepared for you from the foundation of the world; for I was hungry and you gave me food, I was thirsty and you gave me drink, I was a stranger and you welcomed me, I was naked and you gave me clothing, I was sick and you took care of me, I was in prison and you visited me."

Then the righteous will answer him, "Lord, when was it that we saw you hungry and gave you food, or thirsty and gave you something to drink. . . or naked and gave you clothing? And when was it that we saw you sick or in prison and visited you?"

And the king will answer them, "Truly I tell you, just as you have done to the one of the least of these, who are members of my family, you did it to me."(Matt. 25:34-40)

To those who did not welcome the stranger and visit the sick and feed the hungry Jesus said, "You that are accursed depart from me into the eternal fire prepared for the devil and his angels" (Matt. 25: 41).

Those strong words of Jesus leave little doubt that a gospel that does not concern itself with the cries of the poor and the pain of the oppressed is a false gospel. To highlight the seriousness of the offense of devaluing another human being, Jesus prescribed the offense as punishable by being burned in a fire. To hold back from anyone when they are in need, Jesus said, is sin. Jesus gave warning of punishment for those who preach but do not live the gospel. Jesus used the imagery of "burning in a lake of fire" as the kind of punishment that befits those who oppress another person. It is interesting to note that when Jesus used the imagery of "a hell of fire" it was nearly always in the context of the rich oppressing the poor.

A strong affirmation of the authority of Scripture is central for a faithful congregation's ability to preach the good news of the gospel. It is in the Bible that God's salvation history is recorded. The Holy Spirit inspired the words recorded in Scripture, and the life, teachings, death, and resurrection of Jesus as revealed in the Scriptures are the fuel that powers the engine of peace.

However, the good news of the gospel Scripture records becomes bad news when the very institution that God called to preach the good news insulates itself from the world to which it is called to give witness. Whenever the institution becomes overly occupied with protecting the structures that it built around itself then the good news ceases to flow. The structures then become a dam that prevents the ever-flowing stream of the good news of peace to reach out to the parched earth.

A church that is no longer a good news church is concerned that its own image fit well into the culture of the day. It is a church that speaks evil of government when government works for the poor. This church then attempts to make government support its values. The good news becomes bad when the church prescribes certain beliefs as more important than a relationship with God through Jesus Christ. When a people can no longer hear the voice of the Holy Spirit leading them into ministries of justice, then the good news becomes empty and hollow.

To refuse to identify with the poor and walk with them in their journey, seeking relief from their pain and oppression, carries the same penalty as for those who inflict the pain on them. Not to identify with the oppressed is to stand with the oppressor. There is no middle ground to stand on. To search the Scriptures for the purpose of maintaining orthodoxy without practicing hospitality to the stranger leaves the one who searches lean in grace and bankrupt in spirituality. Of course, I am not advocating that we do not study the Scripture. When we identify as well as we can with those in society for whom justice is a stranger, then the Scriptures take on fresh meaning and generate power.

To judge another person for whatever reason without getting to know that person is to devalue that person. Jesus said that to devalue someone, to call them a fool, is to risk punishment in fire. The directive in the Matthew 18 principle is to always go and talk first to the person who is being charged with wrongdoing. Self-righteous Christians who go to other people or church leaders first when someone does not believe as the judgers do become enemies of the gospel.

We cannot hear the cries of the poor if we only talk about them. If we do not hear their cries, we allow ourselves to believe that we need not walk with them. If we do not walk with them, we can never hear their pain. God will lead faithful people in the paths of those who suffer injustice. Together they will be able to walk on the sharp stones of the narrow path.

The longer I lived in the city the more I needed to search the Scriptures to find a direction for ministry. The more I read the Bible, the more I discovered that the pages were pregnant with the gospel waiting to be born in the life of a oppressed community. I will not live long enough or have enough experience in a variety of cultures to glean all that is true. I will never get old enough not to find new applications of the good news I heard preached as a boy in Zurich, Ontario.

The congregation that nurtured me in my early years taught me to take the Scriptures seriously. That gift I shall always treasure. The first Scripture I committed to memory was John 3:16: "For God so loved the world that he gave his only Son, so that everyone who believes in him may not perish but have eternal life." I also heard many sermons based on 1 John 2:15: "Do not love the world or the things in the world. The love of the Father is not in those who love the world."

I never could reconcile those two passages. On the one hand if God loved the world would it not be right that we also love the world? Were the preachers wrong who insisted that we must be a people separated from the world? To be separated meant that we dressed differently, refrained from going to certain places (like bars or dance halls), and avoided being influenced in the ways of the world through TV and radio.

When I got out into the "world" where the real drama of life was being played, I needed an anchor. The anchor for me became the assurance that if God loves the world, then I can freely love that world. God also loves me as a part of God's world. But I needed to find ways to love the world as God loves the world. I am still in the process of finding acceptable ways to live out my faith in that world God loves, a world calling out to be loved by all of God's children.

As I walked the streets of the city, saw the broken-down houses, looked into the empty eyes of children, witnessed the devastation of substance abuse, observed the inferior educational opportunities, brushed against police brutality, heard the noise of churches indifferent to the needs of the community, counseled with fragmented families, looked into the business end of a gun, stood by the coffins of murder victims, I often wondered where God was.

If God loves the world, why do these conditions exist? Why this dehumanization? Does God not have power to silence corrupt politicians? Can God not force absentee landlords to repair houses they rent to the poor? Can't God make things come out fair? Why do mothers have to resort to prostitution to get money to feed their children? Why do churches that preach about God's love not live out the gospel of love?

I remember reading in the same newspaper two stories. One story was of a boy in another city being sentenced to two years in prison for stealing candy bars. The other was a story of someone embezzling millions of dollars and some lawyers persuading a judge to set that man free. Where was God? I wondered. Is there nothing fair in this world!

When I came to neighborhoods where only the wealthy could live, I again questioned God. Why are these people spared the pain of my inner city friends? Why do they have better schools for their children? When they are sick, why do they have to go to the crowded hospital wards in the city where roaches crawl on the floor?

I have learned since that my questions about the wealthy were not appropriate questions. There also was pain in the wealthy community. There were wealthy people who cared about the poor and worked hard and diligently to bring hope. In fact some wealthy people who professed no religion cared more deeply about justice than some Christians who displayed their religion like a garland of flowers around their neck.

I remember having been called by a funeral director who requested me to officiate at a funeral for a seven-year-old girl. The little girl lived with her mother, several aunts, and a grandmother only few blocks away from the church. I inquired as to details of the tragedy. They told me the story of the child's death. The body of the girl was found in an alley about four miles from where the family lived. She apparently had been abducted, sexually molested, and left dead in the alley. I discovered later that the little girl lived in an apartment shared by twenty-three other people. She was gone from home more than two days before the rest of the household missed her.

I do not recall the text I used for the funeral. I do recall some of my feelings. I felt anger. Anger at the family for neglecting their own child. Anger at the perpetrator of such a heinous crime. Anger at a system that destroyed families. How could a loving God allow conditions to exist where pain of this magnitude is inflicted on human beings!

But I have long since stopped blaming God for what is wrong in the world. If I have a little pain over sin and suffering, God has much pain. The story of the first people in the garden suggests God gave humans authority over creation:

> God blessed them and God said to them, "Be fruitful and multiply, and fill the earth and subdue it; and have dominion over the fish of the sea and over the birds of the air and over every living thing that moves upon the face of the earth." God said, "See, I have given you every

plant yielding seed . . . and every tree with seed in its fruit; you shall have them for food. And to every beast of the earth, and to every bird of the air, and to everything that creeps on the earth, every thing that has the breath of life, I have given every green plant for food." And it was so. (Gen. 1: 28-30)

It is the will of God that everyone share in the bounties of the earth. But when the earth's caretakers get greedy and horde for themselves more then they need then another will go hungry. James said in greed are the seeds of war.

It seems to me that it is a sin of greater magnitude to offend another human being than to offend God. Humans are such fragile creatures. They can be broken beyond repair. God is strong and forgiving. Humans cannot always find it within themselves to forgive. They carry the heavy load of anger and bear the pain that goes with an unforgiving spirit. There is nothing as powerful to destroy inner peace as harboring a grudge and refusing to forgive another. When we offend God, God offers us forgiveness. God forgives and remembers our sins no longer. Humans cannot forget.

An unforgiving spirit prevents healing of injury caused by injustice. It's like creating a snow person after a wet snow blanket covers the lawn. As a small snowball is rolled into a giant lump of snow, it gathers trash and dirt. When the snow person is carefully constructed, with a carrot for a nose and a lump of coal for eyes and a hat and a scarf, it awaits the sun. As it is exposed to the sun, the snow melts and the trash and dirt are all that remain. An unforgiving spirit will melt away the quality of life God intends for all people—and what remains, again, will be the trash and the dirt.

I recall many times walking through the neighborhood surrounded by houses so badly in need of repair I wondered if God did not care for people who had no other place to live.

One winter, in a nine-block area, a total of nineteen children perished in house fires. Most of the fires were caused by bad wiring or unsafe heating stoves. The absentee landlords were always there on time to collect the rent. But when repairs needed be made, the landlords were hard to find.

I complained to one landlord about sewage in a basement and said if not repaired I would report it to the city health department. "If you do, I'll run you out of town," he responded. My appreciation for his reply was not the most generous.

Some months later that landlord's office was robbed, and he was shot dead. I reflected on my relationship with him. For a fleeting moment when I read the news of his death I wanted to say, "Serves him right." But putting one person down thinking it will pull another up never produces healing or hope. It only puts one on the same level as the person being put down. Those who do violence to others are also people with deep hurts and scars. That landlord was a person loved by God. "It served him right" was as wrong as his exploiting the poor.

How could I have contacted him about the sewer without invoking his hostility? My approach closed the door to dialogue. I could smell the sewage in the basement but did not open myself to learn what pain may have been inside of him.

That is not to justify the unscrupulous action of a landlord but to recognize that when we hurt another, we also hurt ourselves. The civil rights movement was not only to free African-Americans and restore their dignity but also to free racists from the prison of hate and prejudice enslaving them.

In his inaugural address, recorded in Luke 4, Jesus said,

> The Spirit of the Lord is upon me,
>   because he has anointed me
>   to bring good news to the poor.
> He has sent me to proclaim
> release to the captives
>   and recovery of sight to the blind,
>   to let the oppressed go free,
> to proclaim the year of the Lord's favor.
> (Luke 4:18,19)

Any successful business or institution has a mission statement. The Luke 4 passage became mine. For me the only trustworthy foundation for ministry is focused through the life and teaching of Jesus. I am thinking here not of the baby Jesus but of the man Jesus, who called into question self-serving religious institutions; the Jesus who broke down traditions and talked to the Samaritan women at the well; the Jesus who ate and drank with sinners and ministered to the prostitutes; the Jesus who always had the capacity to forgive and heal.

In my continuing search for ways the church could begin to address the pain and dehumanization evident in St. Louis, I again listened. I spent many hours with Macler Shepard, sitting in his furniture repair shop on Sheridan Avenue imagining what this community could again become.

Macler is an unusual man. His astute insights into the political system were not appreciated by those who used the system for their own self-interest. His furniture repair shop became a shop to repair broken people. The welfare mother could always get a listening ear and some advice on how to cope with the problems with her teenage boys. Senior citizens who needed help always went to Macler first. In prayer meetings and Bible studies, one could expect to hear wise sayings from Macler. I recall his saying one time that "We talk the gospel by the mile and walk it by the inch."

When young men needed jobs, Macler would counsel them to be the best person they could be, regardless of their position: "If you are the janitor," he would tell them, "be the best janitor you can be." He usually warned them not to try to start from the top of the ladder: "If you fall from the top of the ladder, you could fall hard."

During the 1960s, Lady Bird Johnston had a dream to beautify the country. Every city was encouraged to appoint a Beautification Committee. St. Louis chose the nineteenth ward, the area in which our church was located, as the target area for the beautification program. The goals were to clean alleys, paint fences, and plant flowers. A meeting by invitation was called to appoint this committee.

Macler did not get an invitation because the politicians could not count on him to promote their special interests. I was asked to chair the committee. I immediately involved Macler, and he became the real leader while I served as designated leader. I did not know the community; he did. Macler taught me how to walk alongside a leader who knew the road. That journey has lasted nearly forty years. Evangelism is not selling a product or marketing some commodity. It is walking beside another in a trust relationship that lasts a lifetime.

Macler never knew something good could not be accomplished. With his leadership, over one thousand houses were built or reconstructed as homes for families who had never before lived in a safe house. A shoe factory was brought into the area to provide jobs. A clinic was established, and about twenty doctors in the city volunteered time to address community health needs. A Head Start program was established for the little children and a reading program for adults.

I was told by religious institutions I approached for money to rebuild houses that the church was not in the real estate business. When I asked organizations that worked with peace and justice issues, their concern was that a theological study be done first. When I talked to people with expertise in mission and evangelism, they told me there was nothing in the area worth saving.

But there were people there. Many people. There are no people not loved by God. The very people we judge may well be the real people of God. The people who do not always act like us may behave more like kingdom people than we do.

God's purpose is usually accomplished by the most unlikely people. What did young David the shepherd boy know about being king? Why did God call Moses the murderer to go back to Egypt to lead Israel out of bondage? Why did God call Saul, who persecuted the Christians, to become a leader and spokesman for the beginning of the church? Of all twelve disciples Jesus chose, likely not one would make it past the first interview with a pastoral search committee.

When the church does not respond to cries for justice, God often finds another way. On Jesus' march to Jerusalem, the religious community wanted the people to refrain from shouting praise to God. Jesus said that the very stones would cry out if the people remained silent. If the church is silent when the cry goes out for justice, then God uses the "stones" to accomplish God's purpose.

My faith in institutions needed repair after many rejections of requests for financial help to test whether houses falling down could be fixed. But one day a person visited the neighborhood where his grandparents once lived. He asked if there was anything he could do to help restore the houses in the community. Macler Shepard told him about his dream of rehabilitating houses. The next day Tom DePew came with a check to do one house. Tom made it clear that his motive was not religious. For me this was a message that when the church does not respond, God will find another way.

Tom became not only a partner in the community organization but also a loved and trusted friend. He was not loved because he gave money; he was loved because he cared enough to become a friend. His caring was by action, not by words. His gift to do one house was followed by many more. While Tom did not verbalize his faith very frequently, in many conversations with him I could sense a deep inner faith that moved him to be salt and light in the world.

I must hasten to say that denominational structures did become involved. They gave substantial loan money. People came to live and work in the area. It became crucial to me to overcome my first negative response to the church I loved. My faith in the church was restored by people like Cecil and Judy Miller, who came to the city to teach but soon gave all their time to work with Macler in community organization. The

Mennonite Disaster Service men, over three hundred, who came to help with the housing project also restored my faith.

Grace Knechtel and Rachael Albrecht, who lived in the area for many years, gave faithful witness that God loves the world. Grace was an unusual person. Trained in nursing the body, she also nursed the spirit of many people,. A Canadian, she had a deep inner calling to be God's servant, ministering to whomever God led in her path. For nearly twenty years she lived in the community and in her free time conducted Bible classes with children. She was always active in the church and community programs. She practiced her nursing profession at Barnes Hospital. When she worked the late shift, she took the bus home and walked several blocks through the crime-ridden community without ever being accosted. She was loved and protected by the community and by her faith in God.

Rachel was also a nurse. She too was loved by the community and gave herself to be God's witness of love and peace. Her many gifts enriched the life of the church and the community. Both Grace and Rachel will be fondly remembered as long as one person is still alive who knew them.

Cecil and Judy Miller brought with them special gifts. Besides being caring and concerned about justice and peace, they had gifts to match their convictions. I often think of them and give thanks for their friendship and the mentoring they offered me. I must also mention Ron Alderfer as one of many volunteers who spent a summer or more in community service. And Mary Rittenhouse volunteered for two summers in a Head Start program. Some twenty-five years later, Mary became my wife. I hesitate to mention such few names, because so many more people invested their lives to work for justice. Indeed God's people in the community and in the church were who kept my faith in God and the church alive.

Chapter 3

Jesus, Justice, and Darlene

WHILE WALKING THE GLASS-STREWN STREETS, and meeting barking dogs emerging from derelict cars, I often wondered who Jesus is and was. Was Jesus really a person who cared about justice? Was Jesus the person of whom the churches sang every Sunday? Was Jesus that baby portrayed in the children's Christmas pageant? Was he the one Isaiah talked about when he wrote,

> For a child has been born for us,
>   a son given to us;
> authority rests upon his shoulders;
>   and he is named
> Wonderful Counselor, Mighty God,
>   Everlasting Father, Prince of Peace.
> His authority shall grow continually,
>   and there shall be endless peace
> for the throne of David and his kingdom.
>   He will establish and uphold it with justice and
>   with righteousness
>   from this time and for ever more.
> (Isa. 9:6, 7)

When the angels and a multitude of the heavenly host announced Jesus' birth, they sang, "Glory to God in the highest heaven and on earth peace among those whom he favors." Did they announce that Jesus' mission was one of peacemaking? If he was the "prince of peace," it would be a fair assumption that he would be concerned that there be peace and justice for all people.

Isaiah also said that if there is no justice, there will be no peace. The book of Isaiah is laced with passages referred to as prophecies of a Messiah coming to deliver justice. He would deliver salvation through forgiveness of sin.

Jesus was criticized one time for healing a person and pronouncing his sins forgiven. His faultfinders were offended when he forgave the person's sins. I treasure the story recorded by Luke of Jesus being in a room filled with Pharisees and scribes. Jesus had been working signs and wonders in the community. Many people gathered in a house to hear him teach. In fact the room was so full no more people could get in. Some loyal people came with a paralytic they wanted Jesus to heal. They soon discovered that the room was too full, so they needed to devise another way to get him to Jesus. They decided to take him up on the roof, open some tile, and let him down in front of Jesus.

My imagination cannot fully fathom the scene that unfolded as they worked to get the man to Jesus, but what I can glimpse is fascinating. Imagine sitting in the room, spellbound at what Jesus is saying, when without warning dust and dirt start falling. Jesus' listeners are likely more then a little annoyed. Then all of a sudden this paralyzed man hanging on some ropes is lowered right in front of where Jesus is sitting. Most likely the people in the room recognize this man, whom they probably label unclean. When Jesus sees the faith of the friends of the paralytic, he pronounces the paralytic's sins forgiven.

But the Pharisees take offense at Jesus for forgiving sins. Only God can forgive sins is their response to what they are witnessing. The Pharisees and the scribes are highly insulted when Jesus' reply suggests that indeed he can forgive sin. And adding insult to injury is the idea that healing of body and forgiving of sins are equal acts of God.

Justice has something to do with making wrong things right. It speaks to issues of people being denied what is intended for their welfare, as the Pharisees and scribes sought to deny the healing and forgiveness Jesus offered the paralytic. Justice is denied when persons are discriminated against because of how they were created by God. It has something to do with abuse of power. It confronts situations where evil is condoned so an institution can stay alive.

Justice speaks word of judgment when bad decisions are paraded as truth and people are crushed by ambitious tyrants in a mad rush for power; when reaching for the top of the ladder justifies trampling on people on the rung below; when greed takes away food from the mouths of little children; when perpetrators of war are called "peacemakers"; when pain is inflicted on innocent persons; when lies are told to devalue another; when a person is held captive by someone who feels superior.

The Jesus I learned about in my first years in Sunday school was not, however, the Jesus of justice, nor was that Sunday school Jesus really a Jesus who would capture the imagination of an oppressed community. Among the oppressed in St. Louis, manger scenes with a happy family surrounded by angels on a cold winter night did not carry the same meaning as the reality of a child hungry, cold, without "angels." The Joseph beside the baby seemed strange to the mother giving birth not knowing where the child's father was. The wise men who brought precious gifts including gold did not come to welfare parents. The "shepherds" that came to welfare children came not to worship but to steal.

Philip Yancey speaks eloquently in his book *The Jesus I Never Knew.* He reports that

> the more I studied Jesus, the more difficult it became
> to pigeon-hole him. He said little about the Roman oc-

cupation, the main topic of conversation among his countrymen, and yet he took a whip to drive out petty profiteers from the Jewish temple. He urged obedience to the Mosaic law while acquiring the reputation as a lawbreaker. He could be stabbed with sympathy for a stranger, yet turn on his best friend with the flinty rebuke, "Get behind me Satan!" He had uncompromising views on rich men and loose women, yet both enjoyed his company.

I am not advocating that we discontinue dramatizing the events around the birth of Jesus. Rather I am urging a deeper and more honest search for the meaning of the man Jesus. How do his birth, his teaching by words and actions, the company he kept, the people he called to follow him, and his death and resurrection tell us what God was doing through him?

It is important to hear the story of Jesus' mother as she proclaims her insight as to who this child was that she was carrying in her body. On her was bestowed the honor of giving birth to a boy and then training and preparing her son to be the Savior of the world. When God chose Mary to be the mother of the Savior, he also gave her spiritual wisdom and understanding of God's purpose for the Savior to come into the world. One day while Mary was visiting with her cousin Elizabeth, she broke into ecstatic language. Under the power of the Spirit, she spoke like Hannah did upon the dedication of her son Samuel. As Luke 1:46-53 records, Mary said,

> "My soul magnifies the Lord,
>   and my spirit rejoices
> in God my Savior,
> for he has looked with favor on
>   the lowliness of his servant.
> Surely, from now on
>   all generations will call me blessed;
> for the Mighty One has done great things for me,
>   and holy is his name.

His mercy is for those who fear him
　　from generation to generation.
He has strength with his arm;
　　he has scattered the proud
　　　　in the thoughts of their hearts.
He has brought down the
　　powerful from their thrones,
　　and lifted up the lowly;
he has filled the hungry with good things,
　　and sent the rich away empty."

Mary understood that Jesus' ministry had something to do with justice. Social leveling was part of justice. Those who used their power selfishly would lose their power, and those who were powerless would gain power. The hungry people would be fed, but the greedy ones who accumulated an overabundance would go hungry.

Mary must have been familiar with the many Isaiah passages calling for a time of renewal and refreshing. Jesus' ministry was to be a time when good news came to those who were forced to live with bad news. Jesus' coming was an introduction to a way of peace that called for wars to cease. The good news would be that of the lion and lamb eating together, not eating each other, of a time when vipers would no longer sting little children, when bounties of the earth would be shared equally with all, when one nationality would not be favored over another, when all cultures would reflect God's love and beauty and enrich each other. Mary dreamed of a time when love would overshadow evil.

Luke talks about a man well advanced in age called Simeon who cared about justice. He was serving in the temple when Jesus' parents brought Jesus to do what was customary under the law. The Holy Spirit revealed to Simeon that he should see the Messiah yet in his lifetime. When he saw the baby Jesus, he took him in his arms and praised God:

> "Master, now you are dismissing
>   your servant in peace,
>   according to your word;
> for my eyes have seen your salvation,
>   which you have prepared in
>   the presence of all peoples,
> a light for revelation to the Gentiles
>   and for glory to your people Israel."
> (Luke 2:29-32)

Simeon longed for the kind of justice that would not discriminate between Gentiles and Jews. He believed salvation was for all people who were created by God. The good news of the Messiah brought calmness and peace to him. Now, he proclaimed, "I am ready to die."

In my reading of the Scriptures I searched for a Jesus that made sense in the inner city. The story of Jesus' baptism and his forty days in the wilderness began to open a window for me as to what the good news was all about. John the Baptist had been preaching a baptism of repentance and forgiveness of sins. He announced that another person would follow him whose shoes he was not worthy to untie.

John leaned hard on the prophesies of Isaiah, who wrote of the one that should come to prepare the way for the Messiah:

> "The voice of one crying out
>   in the wilderness:
> Prepare the way of the Lord,
>   make his paths straight.
> Every valley shall be filled
>   and every mountain and hill
>   shall be made low,
> and the crooked shall be made straight,
>   and the rough ways made smooth;
> and all flesh shall see the salvation of God."
> (Luke 3:4-6)

The salvation of God was announced by a voice when Jesus came to John for baptism. Luke records this story.

Now when all the people were baptized, and when Jesus also had been baptized and was praying, the heaven was opened and the Holy Spirit descended upon him in bodily form like a dove. And a voice came from heaven, "You are my Son, the Beloved; with you I am well pleased." (Luke 3:21, 22)

There is some significance to the fact that following the baptism Jesus went out into a desert place for forty days. Luke records that Jesus was full of the Holy Spirit when he left the Jordan and was led by the Spirit into the wilderness. I assume Jesus needed time to reflect and to sort out what his ministry should encompass. Jesus was as human as we are. Likely his life plan was not all neatly scripted. He had choices to make. Jesus' days in the desert were a time for him to think about those decisions and to wait on the Spirit of God to direct him. That is not unlike what all followers of Jesus experience. We need to take time out to listen what the Spirit is saying to us.

Jesus must have had to think carefully, because he had many options for doing good deeds. I have heard pastors say that the Spirit tells them what to say when they are in the pulpit, implying that to prepare ahead of time is to not depend on the Holy Spirit. While Jesus was empowered by the Spirit, I think he still did some careful planning as he developed his ministry. Even as good preaching requires hard work in preparation to say more accurately and carefully what God wants spoken, so Jesus worked even harder.

Jesus, knowing his ministry would only be for a short time, needed to be sure he was addressing the kingdom message God sent him to communicate. At some point the tempter came to detract Jesus from God's primary purpose for his ministry. I don't know in what form the tempter may have come. Perhaps it was as a spirit being, someone from another planet, a Pharisee being used by the tempter who came out into the desert to talk Jesus into moving his ministry in a direction that would short-circuit what God's call was for him. I guess it doesn't really matter. The fact is that the tempter came to Jesus.

The tempter came with three crucial tasks for Jesus. The first temptation had to do with making bread. There was poverty in the land. There were people who longed to have some bread for their empty stomachs. The Scriptures speak a great deal about bread and feeding hungry people. Jesus replied to the tempter's bread-making urgings, "It is written, 'One does not live by bread alone.'" Jesus' call from heaven was not to be only a bread maker. It is noteworthy, however, that among the first things Jesus did in his ministry was to make bread and feed the multitudes.

The next temptation has something to do with the political structures. There was anger and unrest over the Roman jurisdiction of the land. The Zealot party was gaining strength in protesting the injustice experienced under the powers of Rome. Surely it would have been a worthy cause for Jesus to become involved in the political process and restore justice and peace for the people of Israel. But Jesus said no to the tempter's request to focus his ministry around the political injustices of the day. Jesus no doubt could have given political leadership and restore a sense of hope back to the people.

Jesus' ministry did have some political implications. When Jesus chose his disciples he included Zealots. It was the Zealots who wanted to overthrow the power of Rome. Throughout Jesus' ministry he was a threat to the political system. One time he called Herod a fox. He had some harsh and unkind words to say regarding those who exercised oppressive power over other people. Finally he died a political prisoner's death.

The third temptation was the ace the tempter carried up his sleeve. I suspect the tempter did not really expect Jesus to buy into the first two options. But the third one was the bell ringer. The tempter takes Jesus to Jerusalem to the pinnacle of the temple. The pinnacle represented the highest point of power in the religious system. The tempter was suggesting to Jesus, "Your ministry is here in the religious community." The temptation seems to have been that Jesus could have been the chief of all chiefs in the religious institution. "If you jump, the people will catch you."

Like the poverty in the land and the disarray in the political structures, the religious community was also messed up. Jesus said no to the temple temptation with the same authority he had demonstrated in rejecting bread-making and political involvement. But it is interesting to note that the very first activity he engaged in was to go to the synagogue where he grew up. Jesus was given the scroll and invited to read the lesson from the Scriptures. He read from Isaiah 61, taking that occasion to announce, through Isaiah, what his ministry was all about. He did not yield to the temptations to compartmentalize his call from God. To move in any direction other than what was God's intention for him would have made God's plan for the salvation of his people null and void.

Jesus introduced a ministry like a rainbow arching, after a spring storm, over all of life. Every person from every nation was to be welcomed into the kingdom. No one because of color of skin, origin, or how God created her or him was to be excluded. The ministry Jesus was called to was one that did not divide soul from spirit. Jesus saw people as whole beings; all their needs were to be respected.

I would not trust a person to minister to my spiritual needs who would not also take seriously my physical needs. One would be hard pressed to make a case from the teachings of Jesus that it is more important to minister to the spiritual than to the physical. Long debates, however, could be engaged in to prove or disprove that statement. An argument might be that we have the body only for a short time but the spirit is for eternity. Might one then rephrase the words of John, "How can you minister to that which you cannot see when you do not minister to that which you can see?"

My intent is not to devalue the need to call people to faith. It is only to value in greater depth the need for justice here and now. A careful study of some of the great revival movements of history would reveal that spiritual renewal happened as a result of someone taking seriously the call from Jesus to start ministering through a "cup of cold water."

In reading the lesson from the scroll, Jesus was initiating his inaugural address. He claimed the Isaiah 61 reading as his call and God's purpose for sending him into the world, exclaiming that "The Spirit of the Lord is upon me. . . . to proclaim the year of the Lord's favor" (Luke 4:18, 19).

The year of the Lord's favor might more accurately be rendered the year of jubilee, a year viewed as set aside by God as a time to proclaim liberty to all the inhabitants of the land. Jubilee emphasized the sacredness of all of God's creation. The land that sustained all living creatures was to be fallow for two years, suggesting that all natural resources should be honored and cared for. Real property was to revert back to its original owner. Debts were to be forgiven, and those compelled by poverty to sell themselves for indentured service to their brothers were to be released. The year of Jubilee called for social leveling because all people are of equal value before God. The law of Jubilee prevented any one family from gaining excessive power and control.

Following the reading of the Isaiah text, Jesus said, "Today this Scripture has been fulfilled in your hearing." While Jesus said no to all three temptations, his life and ministry nevertheless did touch on bread-making, political confrontation, and religious ministry. His religious ministry included calling people to repentance and forgiveness of sin. Jesus told Nicodemus that he must be born from above. Jesus called people on a new spiritual journey. He said that the journey is on a narrow road. It is for those who seek first the kingdom of God. To walk on the narrow road required a death to a kind of spiritual practice that disregarded justice and compassion. Jesus said no to the tempter because the good news Jesus was bringing had something to do with bread-making; it had something to do with the political structures; it had something to do with spirituality. It was to announce Jubilee. To place all the emphasis on only one of these would not be good news.

Jesus was not about to let any one detract him from God's purpose for his mission. The tempter would have won the victory could he have persuaded Jesus to isolate one area of ministry at the expense of the others. The three were of equal importance. One could not place a higher value on spiritual ministry than on bread-making for hungry people. That is not to even hint that spiritual nurture and establishing or renewing right relationship with God is not important. It is only to say that the biblical mandate is to feed hungry people and stand in the gap when evil keeps justice away from hungry people.

Luke records the early ministry of John the Baptist. John's mission was to prepare the way for the Messiah. Isaiah was inspired by God to envision the future and write a job description for John the Baptist. The job description, as earlier noted, was to "prepare the way of the Lord, make his paths straight."

John was the door opener for Jesus to enter into his calling. John's message was a call to repentance for the forgiveness of sin. The crowds came to him to be baptized. John spoke hard words to them. He told them that their origin of birth and family lineage was not a paved road to God. He told them they must bear fruit that reflects repentance. The crowd asked John, "What then must we do?" John replied that "Whoever has two coats must share with anyone who has none, and whoever has food must do likewise." The Scriptures consistently link caring for needs of people with salvation. Only one time did Jesus tell someone he needed to be "born from above." Meanwhile countless times he emphasized doing justice and caring for the needy.

As I earlier mentioned, Matthew records the words of Jesus when Jesus gave his dissertation on the judgment of the nations. Jesus told the story of the king who would welcome all those on his right hand who had offered him clothing, food, care. When they asked when they had done this, the king would "answer them, 'Truly I tell you, just as you did it to one of the least of these who are members my of my family, you did it to me'" (Matt. 25:34-40). That story goes on to say that those who did not care about the physical needs of people were punished and denied entrance into God's eternal reward. When Jesus talks about not doing justice, there is always a penalty to follow.

The stories of Jesus' early ministry were accounts of making bread, healing sick people, making wine out of water, casting out demons, and calling a band of disciples to follow him. Later in his ministry, Jesus prayed for his disciples:

> "I have given them your word, and the world has hated them because they do not belong to the world, just as I do not belong to the world. I am not asking you to take them out of the world, but I ask you to protect them from the evil one. . . . Sanctify them in the truth; your word is truth. As you have sent me into the world, so I have sent them into the world." (John 17:14-18)

As I read those Scriptures in the heat of the Vietnam War and the civil rights movement, the incarnation theology began to make sense. "The word became flesh and dwelt among us," began to take on meaning for me.

Now if the followers of Jesus are sent into the world even as he was sent into the world to bring good news, how do the followers become good news bearers? How is the presence of Jesus realized by people who suffer from injustice? Being human, every one of us experiences times of being treated unfairly. Where is God when there is unfairness? Is God there when there is fear? When there is poverty and hunger is God there to make bread and turn the water into wine? A friend of ours recently died from a debilitating cancer. She was recognized by many of her friends as a saintly woman. Was it fair that she needed to finish her last days on earth with her body wasting away?

Could God not intervene when humans make war against each other and kill innocent people? Was there no way that God could have stopped the insanity and evil of the murder of millions of people during the Holocaust?

The Jesus who prayed to God, "As you have sent me into the world so send I them," also said to the disciples, "Blessed are the peacemakers." The followers of Jesus have an awesome task of being peacemakers in the world. Is not the presence of Jesus best experienced through another person who reaches out to us in our hour of deepest need? Can we become God to one another?

I recall as if it were today receiving a telephone message that a young Sunday school teacher in our congregation had been murdered. The family lived in the Pruitt Igoe Housing Project where we once lived. It was in the heat of the summer and the ferment of the civil rights movement. On receiving the word I immediately went to be with the family. When I got to the project, an angry gang of young men was standing around the entrance to the building. I knew they carried knives and guns. Two murders had taken place a few hours earlier.

Darlene, who was the victim, and her mother had been away all day house hunting. The mother said, "We have to get out of here before someone gets killed." After searching for an apartment all day without success they came home weary. As the last errand of the day, Darlene went to the corner store to get a paper to see if there were any new rental listings. On her return, she encountered a gang shoot-out. A member of the gang grabbed Darlene and used her as a shield. As a result she was shot and killed, along with another gang member. The blood was still on the sidewalk when I got there.

When I drove to the apartment and saw the gang, I could not bring myself to stop. I drove past and decided to try again. Then I drove past again and still sensed too much fear in me to attempt to walk through that gang of angry men. The face of a white person who was not known was unwelcome in that racially tense atmosphere. I don't think I was afraid to die, but for some unknown reason I was not in a big hurry to die yet that night.

I needed to find a way to go through the gang and climb a narrow flight of dark stairs to sixth floor. I was their pastor; I needed to go and be with them in their grief. But I was afraid. It occurred to me to call a friend, another pastor with whom I shared an office. I hurried back to the office and called Don Register. Don came immediately. We got to the building and the gang was still there. Nothing seemed to have changed.

With Don at my side, I walked through the gang without feeling an ounce of fear. The truth of the incarnation became a reality for me. God dwells in human beings. The words of Jesus' prayer, "As you have sent me into the world so sent I them," flashed in my mind with a peace that God is present now even as in Jesus' day. "The word became flesh" for me in Don and calmed my anxious spirit. Don was God for me that day as we climbed six flights of stairs to minister to a grieving family.

Sometimes a God in heaven is too far away. In our hour of peril or fear, we need a God whom we can see, hear, and feel the very breath of love coming from. Love from God flows in its purest form when it conveyed through a human being whose life is committed to the service of God.

I did not answer the question of why there is suffering. Any attempt to do so would be a feeble one at best. Human frailties have no boundaries. There is no hiding place from suffering. God does not inflict suffering on anyone, but being members of the human race makes all of us vulnerable to it. God seeks out people in whom the Spirit of God dwells to be with others in their pain. It is the word becoming flesh and walking with another in their pain that brings hope and makes pain bearable.

When John the Baptist was languishing in prison he began to doubt if Jesus really was the Messiah. His pain in prison seemed greater than his faith. He sent some of his disciples to Jesus to ask him again if he really was the Messiah. Jesus told the disciples to go tell John that "the blind receive their sight, the lame walk, the lepers are cleansed, the deaf hear, the dead are raised, and the poor have good news brought to them. And blessed is anyone who takes no offense at me" (Matt. 11:4-6). That message reassured John that Jesus was the Messiah he claimed to be.

Here, as always, was that ring to Jesus' teaching that included good news to the poor. Jesus taught the disciples to pray that the kingdom would come and that the will of God be done on earth even as it is in heaven. The kingdom of God has something to do with looking to God for daily bread. It has something to do with recognition of the political powers that would prevent the kingdom of heaven on earth. It has something to do with spirituality, the lifeblood of living in the kingdom. As in the Jubilee law of forgiveness of debts, so Jesus encouraged the disciples to pray for forgiveness of debts.

A condition for forgiveness is ability to forgive another who has offended us. Bishop Tutu has spoken eloquently and written forcefully on forgiveness. I wonder how one who has been a victim all his life of racism finds in himself the power to forgive? Bishop Tutu does not gloss over the wrongs done to him. He speaks out with even more boldness over the sin of discrimination. His ability to forgive empowers him to speak with authority. Or how could Nelson Mandela, later the prime minister of South Africa, forgive a nation that held him in prison for more than two decades? Yet an honored guest at Mandela's inauguration was the judge who had sent him to prison.

Given that we are all flawed vessels, often throughout life we will need to seek forgiveness. Unless we forgive, we cannot expect to be forgiven. We cannot remain healthy human beings if we continue to nurse wrongs committed against us. An unforgiving spirit will eventually erode our own self-worth. It creates walls that prevent us from experiencing joy and hope. It gives permission to devalue other people. It can break down our own physical and mental health.

To forgive gives credibility to speak out for justice. To forgive is to be empowered to work with integrity to help change a system before the system destroys itself and hurts many people. Perhaps systems cannot repent, but maybe they can be steered toward improved ability to do "justice, love kindness and walk humbly with God."

I am a bit hesitant to pray that God's will be done on earth as it is in heaven. How is God going to answer that prayer? What if I am expected to be part of the answer? Who of us is ready to lay down our nets and follow him? If we do, what will be the cost?

Jesus said, "Blessed are those who hunger and thirst for righteousness [justice], for they shall be filled." Jesus was more than a prophet, but he also followed in the tradition of a long line of prophets. His message carried the same vein of concerns as that of Amos the herdsman. Amos' time was marked by peace and prosperity. But the prosperity was accompanied by an unprecedented degree of social corruption. Amos was a vigorous spokesman for God's justice and righteousness. He spoke strong words of condemnation to those who had become rich at the expense of others:

> I hate, I despise your festivals,
>   and I take no delight in your solemn assemblies.
> Even though you offer me your burnt offerings
>   and grain offerings,
>   I will not accept them;
> and the offerings of well-being
>   of your fatted animals
>   I will not look upon.
> Take away from me the noise of your songs;

> I will not listen to the melody of your harps.
> But let justice role down like waters,
>   and righteousness like an ever flowing stream.
> (Amos 5:21-24)

Shortly after Amos prophesied to Judah, along came Micah with an equally strong message. His message alternated between warnings of doom and good news of hope. He stressed that God hates idolatry, injustice, and empty rituals. In his message, there is a ring of God's delight in pardoning the penitent. Micah said of Jerusalem and Samaria that they should be destroyed and the cities of Judah doomed. He denounced social evil:

> Alas for those who devise wickedness
>   and evil deed on their beds!
> When the morning dawns, they perform it,
>   because it is in their power.
> They covet fields, and seize them;
>   houses, and take them away;
> they oppress householder and house,
>   people and their inheritance.
> Therefore thus says the Lord:
> now, I am devising against this family an evil
>   from which you cannot remove your necks;
> and you shall not walk haughtily,
>   for it will be an evil time.
> (Micah 2:1-3)

Micah followed his scathing condemnation with a promise to the faithful remnant:

> I will surely gather all of you, O Jacob,
>   I will gather the survivors of Israel;
> I will set them together
>   like sheep in a fold
> like a flock in its pasture;
>   it will resound with people.
> (Micah 2:12)

He then addressed the wicked rulers:

> Listen, you heads of Jacob
>> and rulers of the house of Israel!
> Should you not know justice?—
>> you who hate the good and love the evil,
> who tear the skin off my people,
>> and the flesh off their bones. . . .
> (Micah 3:1, 2)

When Micah spoke to the prophets of the day, he had even stronger words of condemnation. The "powers that be" can advance their evil if given sanction by the religious establishment. So Micah came down hard on the prophets who supported the oppression of the people:

> Thus says the Lord concerning prophets
>> who lead my people astray,
> who cry "Peace" when they have something to eat,
> but declare war against those
>> who put nothing in their mouths.
> Therefore it shall be night to you, without vision,
>> and darkness to you, without revelation.
> The sun will go down upon the prophets,
>> and the day shall be black over them;
> the seers shall be disgraced,
>> and the diviners put to shame;
> they shall all cover their lips,
>> for there is no answer from God.
> (Micah 3:5-7)

Whenever there is repentance and obedience, security can be found. Micah invited turning back to God:

> "Come, let us go up to the mountain of the Lord,
>> to the house of the God of Jacob;
> that he may teach us his ways
>> and that we may walk in his paths."
> For out of Zion shall go forth instruction,

and the word of the Lord from Jerusalem.
He shall judge between many peoples,
    and shall arbitrate between
        strong nations far away;
they shall beat their swords into plowshares,
    and their spears into pruning hooks;
nation shall not lift up sword against nation,
    neither shall they learn war any more;
but they shall all sit under their own vines
        and under their own fig trees,
    and no one shall make them afraid;
        for the mouth of the Lord of hosts has spoken.
(Micah 4:2-4)

As Micah rehearsed the history of how God brought Israel out of slavery and the wilderness, he reminded them of the saving acts of God. Then he asked what God would require of a people ready to obey God:

"With what shall I come before the Lord,
    and bow myself before God on high?
Shall I come before him with burnt offerings,
    with calves a year old?
Will the Lord be pleased with thousands of rams,
    with ten thousand rivers of oil?
Shall I give my firstborn for my transgression,
    the fruit of my body for the sin of my soul?"
He has told you, O mortal, what is good;
    and what does the Lord require of you
but to do justice, and to love kindness,
    and to walk humbly with your God?
(Micah 6:6-8)

In Micah's time the rich were getting richer and the poor had less and less. Power was in the hands of a few. The rich had the power to take away the property of the poor. The prophets gave their support for injustice to run unrestrained in the land. The political system and its rulers thrived on their corruption. The worship of the religious community offered only meaningless ceremonies. The people had forgotten their deliverance from slavery in Egypt.

Meanwhile Jesus came into a time in history that might well be described as similar to the time of Micah. And the stories on the front pages of our newspapers today suggest that our time is not unlike the times of Micah or Jesus.

False prophets today still devalue those unlike themselves and make no effort to understand their history, culture, and values. Slavery could not have lasted as long as it did without support from pulpits on Sundays. Some Christian churches are the greatest offenders in discriminating against people not of European decent, a problem that has only grown worse since the United States declared war on terrorism. Church leaders, whose calling is to speak truth, speak lies about persons created by a loving God and given a natural affection toward persons of the same sex. The church has not yet arrived at the tollgate for its sin of devaluing people who are not like them.

But Micah told the people that, despite all the wrongs there are in the world, there still is hope. The message today in a fragmented world must be a message of hope. Where there is no voice for justice there is no hope. The message of Jesus was a message of hope. God has throughout history kept giving special gifts to the people. He gave Abraham as a blessing to the whole world. God gave the prophets to call God's people back to repentance when they strayed far away. God loved the created world so much that the best gift God could give was God's very Son, Jesus Christ.

Since Jesus' ministry was so short, God was preparing another gift: the church. The Holy Spirit now dwells in and among those who have chosen to be obedient to God's call for salvation. It is through the church now that God wants to bless the world. The church is not the structures labeled *church*. The church is not a building with a steeple. The church is the people in whom the Spirit of God dwells.

Chapter 4

Fear at Midnight
and Structures For Justice

AFTER FIFTEEN YEARS IN THE INNER CITY, weathering the fall-out of the Vietnam War and the civil rights movement, I was ready for a break. I don't remember many days I did not enjoy my work as pastor. Of course some days were more energy enriched than others. There was danger in the streets and good reason for fear. But I never lived in fear. I did live cautiously and exercised as much good judgment as I knew how. Fear and effective ministry are not good bedfellows. Of course I need to admit to times of fear. But I'm not aware that I ever was immobilized by fear.

I recall receiving a call at midnight to come to the bedside of a dying member of our congregation. I had uneasy moments as I walked from the car to the house in a community I did not know and where no one knew me. It is a strange feeling to be some place where nobody knows you. I recall arriving at the airport in Christchurch, New Zealand, all by myself. A sudden awareness surrounded me that I didn't know any person in the whole country. It was a lonely feeling.

My fear and anxiety rose higher when I thought about our leaving the city than when I faced tough situations in the community. We had good schools for our children. We loved our friends who became family to us. We loved city life. There were many educational, cultural, and recreational opportunities in the city that a small country town could not offer. The Cardinals baseball team provided courtesy passes to the clergy for all home games. I still am a Cardinal fan. We were anxious about taking our children out of the city school into a school in an affluent community. When we left the city some said to us, "I suppose you are leaving because you want to take the children out of the city schools." The very opposite was true.

But my energy level was at a point that I needed a change of activity. I looked at invitations to serve in another capacity. One was to become staff member of Mennonite Board of Congregational Ministries (MBCM) with responsibility to work at peace and justice education in North American Mennonite congregations. The position appealed to me, since I had a growing belief that the church needs to look through a new set of lenses to focus its ministry. Not that I had the eyeglasses, but I was willing to share my insight with many other people who had their own wisdom but a different outlook than mine. Perhaps there could be a rekindling of excitement in the denomination in doing "God's will on earth as it is in heaven."

Yet I worried about what I would face if I took the position. Would I need to affirm only one narrow set of truths? I pondered this carefully, because no one person ever has *the* formula for effective ministry. The church is made up of many people with varied life experiences, all valuable. All congregations likely have at least tiny viewpoint fractures. Persons in a congregation who insist their interpretation of Scripture and understanding of an issue represents the only right position are like water in the fractures. Cold sets in, the water freezes, and the expanding ice splits the tiny fractures into chasms.

When persons defend their cause by claiming, "My Bible says, . . ." I begin to wonder what lies behind the statement. We have many master craftspeople capable of making the Bible say whatever they think it should say. Fundamentalism boasts of a literal interpretation of the Bible. It amuses me how those same people can get on the bandwagon to justify war when Jesus clearly said, "Love your enemies."

Truth is discerned when the experiences and insights of the group are shared. Truth is much larger then the limited experience of one person. My story plus the stories of other people begin to point toward truth. An honest search of Scripture gives direction to the foundation of truth. Reading the Scriptures through God's eyes alone—something no human can really do—short-circuits the truth.

Through contacts with congregations throughout the church, I was aware that many in the church were not interested in exploring truth because they already had the truth. Did I really want, through MBCM, to get into situations where my story was not welcome? I was being criticized by some for not preaching against interracial marriage. Some took offense at my participation in protest marches. (I really don't like the term *protest marches* but it was a convenient label attached to activity that spoke out against injustice. I prefer to speak of witness for justice and peace.)

Someone said of me one time, "He is a liberal, an activist, and a foreigner." Actually he was right. My Canadian citizenship entitles me to consider myself a foreigner when I am in the United States. In fact my green card titles me as an alien. As for a liberal and an activist, I really don't know what that is. My first reading of a definition of a liberal or an activist certainly could fit the description of Jesus' life and ministry.

I was chastised at one meeting on for telling of an absentee landlord who unjustly treated his tenants. My critic considered that political involvement. I did do things that would fit the description of an activist. Once a poverty-stricken lady was evicted from her apartment. Our efforts to negotiate with the landlord were not welcomed. The sheriff set all her belongings in the street. I participated in moving it all back in once the sheriff was gone.

A person once told me of his concern over the preacher in his church. He said, "We don't hear the gospel any more, all we hear preached is sermons about love, peace, and sharing; we just never hear the gospel any more." Would my ministry in the denomination working at peace and justice issues be interpreted as not preaching the gospel? For me the message of peace and justice was at the heart of the gospel. What good news is there to the ones who suffer injustice if no voice speaks to their needs? When the powerless have no voice, who speaks for them? When there is no one to walk with those who hurt, how will healing come? When the blind need eyes, is there good news when nobody cares? When people came to Jesus with their deepest need, Jesus always had compassion.

That is not to say that a right relationship with God through Christ—which is what my complainant may have viewed as the missing gospel—is not important. Jesus said one time, "I am the way and the truth and the life." Ministering to the spiritual needs of wounded people is an integral part of the gospel. To downplay spiritual need is as offensive as to downplay the need for healing and justice. Many people for whom justice has not been denied do have spiritual wounds.

One does not give a cup of cold water to another because you want something from them in return. The use of gimmicks or bribes to bring people to accepting Christ is not an acceptable way that I can find in the Scriptures. The mandate in Scripture to do evangelism is speaking the open truth. One never enters the back door to sneak in with the gospel. One knocks on the front door and present oneself with a sincere pure message. A cup of cold water is always given for no other reason than that the person is thirsty.

So I did ponder awhile before I accepted the invitation to work for our denomination. I asked myself if I really wanted to be an advocate for issues the majority of the people did not see as important or at least not important enough to be explicitly addressed. But I did accept the invitation to work for

MBCM. During my seven years of MBCM work I received invitations to visit many congregations. Almost without exception, every congregation had a small core of people for whom justice and peace were an important part of the good news of the gospel. I had the privilege to work with persons who, like me, cared about justice and peace.

Not all arrived at the same conclusions I did. Not everyone agreed with my interpretation of issues or of biblical applications that made sense to me. I did not always agree with them. I learned that it became crucial for me to listen to their story. The life stories of many people I worked with were very different from mine. Our differences placed us on an equal basis to work together to move toward a direction of learning how to do God's will on earth as in heaven.

To respect my friends' positions, though different from mine, freed me to not cave in on my own. Sharing our understandings with each other always brought us a little closer to the truth. To defend one's own cause without respectfully listening to the view of one who disagrees with you is to harm the truth, to move farther from truth. When we dig in heels to defend our way of thinking, the result is usually alienation. Often the real issues are skirted in the arguments; winning the argument becomes more important than discerning truth. When winning becomes everything, splits in the church begin to be justified. Most accounts of divisions in the church have been identified as efforts to maintain a "pure" church. In my judgment it would be more accurate to say that the real issue usually is maintaining control and power.

My good wife Mary reminded me that before we were married she once asked what made me angry. She reports that I said, "When someone treats another unjustly." Mary and I vary greatly in ability to cry. Mary can cry when someone gets injured or is devalued. I wish I could cry like that too. It usually takes something like a global catastrophe before I can cry. Even then I would likely not allow myself to see the worst but would tell myself it could have been worse. I have limited patience when good people always see only bad in anything different from their own experience.

I remember three times I cried in public. These times were related to disappointments in church institutions. I can get angry enough at injustice in the secular society to feel like crying, but when it happens in church institutions it carries an even sharper edge. The wound is inflicted more deeply and the healing process takes longer.

A friend of ours who worked for a church institution was fired. From my perspective she was being treat unjustly. I listened to her story of pain and discouragement. She asked me to accompany her to a conference with her employer. As I tried to bring my perspective to the issue, I began to cry. I felt like the biggest cry-baby in the world. I did not understand my own emotional response. If this situation had unfolded in the secular marketplace, I would have been angry but would not have cried. I cried in this case because the very institution was also a part of me. I gave my life to the church institution which I loved and which nurtured me. It was painful for me to feel the injustice toward my friend. It was as though I, being a part of the institution, also carried the heavy load of responsibility for the injustice inflicted on my friend.

One time I cried in public over women being denied leadership in a congregation. When I terminated the pastorate of a congregation, a search committee began a process to find a new pastor. I had been vocal about my own understanding of women in ministry. It became crucial to me that women not be discriminated against in calls to pastoral ministry.

The search committee polled the congregation to determine if a women would be welcome as new pastor. I had completed the sermon that morning, then called for the committee to report its findings to the congregation. The conclusion of the report was that a woman pastor would not be welcomed. Before the benediction, I registered my disappointment with

the outcome. Then I stood there a few more minutes and cried.
I don't really know for sure why I cried. I think it was because
these church members I loved and cared about did not sense
the gravity of their decision. For me it was and is a sin of discrimination to refuse to accept a person whom God has given
the gifts of pastoral ministry.

Another time I cried in public was when Germantown
Mennonite Church was voted out of membership in Franconia Conference. Before the vote was taken to remove the congregation, I shared my convictions and concerns with the body
assembled that day. It was difficult for me to read my statement through my tears.

Despite valued experiences with MBCM, I discovered that
I had a better platform to do education in peace and justice
while I was pastor of a church in the inner city. That is not to
say that the denominational institutions have no integrity. We
need institutions. If we would dismantle all our institutions
we would soon build others that might not be any better than
the ones we discarded. There would be a good possibility that
they would be even less sensitive. The challenge is always to
make the institution serve the people, not the people serve the
institution. In a discussion of a congregation's relationship to
a conference someone said, "We once had congregations that
had a conference. Now we have a conference that has congregations." An institution that has integrity is there to serve its
constituency, not to coerce its constituency to serve the institution.

The best friends of an institution can be its critics. An institution can lose its way. When it becomes bound to a budget
that needs to be balanced, there are some justice issues it cannot appeal to. In a diverse community, it needs to measure
carefully the issues it addresses. It must guard against offending those with the ability to help meet the budget. When tough
issues arise, the institution must to either be silent or come
out on the side of the majority who are in control of power.

An institution cannot pay the prophet to call it to do justice, when doing justice shuts off the pipeline of resources it needs to survive. That often leaves no room in an institution for persons who will speak out boldly on justice issues.

Yet not to speak out boldly is also to be unfaithful. It is unfaithfulness to oneself as well as one's own conviction of what is right and just and what is wrong and evil. It is unfaithful to the institution because the institution cannot be what it could be. The critics provide eyes through which the institution can see and measure the direction it is taking. Critics' eyes also are a mirror reflecting the path the institution once took. The critic can also be a telescope to help the institution more clearly focus on the future.

A critic is not one who simply finds a fault in the system. A healthy critic is motivated by a deep desire to see justice flow like a cool stream through the pasture where the sheep can safely come to drink. The critic can sense when the water is dirty and not desirable for the sheep. The goal of the critic is not to lash out at the system. True critics always speak out of the pain which arises when the system blindly blocks justice and no longer accomplishes its own goals. Not to listen to a voice that calls with urgency to make mid-course corrections almost guarantees that there will be a collision with the obstacles that are in the way.

The critic that I am talking about is not a run-of-the-mill person who makes a hobby out of finding fault with most everything. Faultfinders are as easy to find as fallen leaves in a hardwood forest in November. There is no end to finding people who are always ready to give advice regardless of any knowledge they may have on the subject. They speak out of a selfish motive and not out of a sense of loss. They do not feel connected to that with which they find fault. Their motive is not healing but may involve some kind of personal vendetta. Their real agenda may well have roots in an entirely different arena on which they are playing a deviant game.

I am talking about a critic being a person who has skills and experience in a certain field to discern strengths and weaknesses and give valuable suggestions. The helpful critic speaks not to condemn an institution but to free the institution from condemning itself. Sometimes the critic points out areas that are too painful to touch.

In the political arena, the institution makes decisions regarding what is in an institution's best interests. When it makes wrong decisions that cause pain, it cannot repent. When a nation makes war against another nation, it cannot admit wrong and repent. When it is wrong, the institution needs to rationalize and rearrange the facts to justify its action.

But institutions that are set up to support the mission of the church can repent if they make bad decisions. And as long as any institution is controlled by human beings, it will make some mistakes or at best some less-than-good decisions requiring repentance. When leaders of a church institution cave in to the pressure of any self-interest group and make a binding decision with which they themselves are not in agreement, then the integrity of the institution begins, sadly, to fade away, and repentance is again required.

I worked for ten years for the Mennonite Conference of Eastern Canada as mission minister. I look back at those years with memories of working with a gifted team of church leaders who had a vision of what the church is all about in the world. I was hired to be a staff person for the missions committee to develop new congregations in eastern Canada.

During that time, the church growth movement was finding acceptance and welcome in many circles and the term *church planting* becoming gospel. I never saw my way clearly enough through that movement to fully endorse it. I rationalized, right or wrong, that the church has already been planted. Our task is to be a presence in a community to help the emergence of the church that is already there, to gather together people ready to join in community with other searching people. It has never seemed to me that a sophisticated marketing scheme works to sell the good news. Just because it works to sell soap and cars and Coke, it does not follow that it works to sell the good new of the gospel. I noted in the February 1, 2000, issue of the *The Mennonite* a quote from the *Evangelical Visitor* to the effect that "eighty-two percent of all church plants die before they are a year old."

The Mennonite Conference of Eastern Canada started twenty new congregations from 1979 to 1989. Of those, seventeen have become a significant witness to their community. I am aware of three that did not mature. I have been away long enough not to know what the state of all of them is at present. I know that nearly all of them have grown into strong stable congregations. One reason the Conference efforts produced fruit was that persons giving vision and leadership were a team. We worked together to provide an option for people to become part of a congregation valuing peace, justice, and Christian community and living in obedience to Jesus. Within that teamwork, I could not forget my vision that a congregation can become a special gift from God to its neighbors.

My role as a staff person was to do research into the community and develop proposals for the missions committee to consider. Wise and gifted committee members brought their observations and suggestions to make it a better proposal. In most cases, a budget was attached to the proposal. When it seemed right to all of us to move forward in a program, money seemed to become available. I felt my role was most effective when I was there to share my own vision and listen to the visions of the people in the community.

An important part of my leadership was to support the new leaders of the new congregations. They could benefit somewhat from my experience but even more simply from being encouraged and having someone to reach out to in times of stress. And, to be sure, some stress there likely will be in such settings.

After ten years with the Mennonite Conference of Eastern Canada, I accepted an invitation to be pastor at Spring Mount Mennonite Church in Pennsylvania on a two-thirds time basis, along with working one-third time for Franconia Mennonite Conference. For the conference I was staff person for the peace and justice committee as well as consultant for urban church strategies. Later I also became overseer of a number of congregations.

Franconia Conference, made up of congregations in eastern Pennsylvania as well as a number in Vermont, took seriously its task of developing new congregations. The conference provided a liberal budget to help emerging congregations. The many staff persons who were well qualified and deeply committed to the mission of the church were a delight to work with. Serving Franconia was very different from my experience in Canada. There I was the only staff person for a program nearly the same size as that of Franconia Conference. I am convinced God used both models to promote God's will on earth as in heaven.

When I turned sixty-five, I resigned from the pastorate of Spring Mount Mennonite Church. The time there had been good. In all my years of ministry, I never worked with a kinder group of people then the members of Spring Mount. The fellowship committee could make meals not equaled anywhere to my knowledge. The congregation was small and, I sensed, had a low self image. They had gone through a period of a lot of pain. During my five years there, however, I was rewarded with seeing growth in the congregation.

When I was an overseer of congregations, I would suggest to new pastors that they likely would get to make one significant change in the congregation. I cautioned them not to fritter away their chips on something that would not build up the congregation.

At Spring Mount, the area in which I wanted to make some changes was worship services. I don't know how well I did that, but from my perspective the worship committee that was appointed worked creatively and with integrity.

Before we came, the congregation did a major redecoration of the building. The old pews remained in use, and on a hot sticky day in July the parishioners' clothing would stick to the pews. There was a strong consensus that we needed new pews. I campaigned for chairs so the the worship services could be enhanced by an ability to rearrange the seating. I had no idea that the change from pews to chairs could become a major issue. But happily the process created no division in the church and led to the conclusion that chairs would be desirable.

It seemed to me they aided a great deal in making the Sunday meetings friendlier. In the church where I grew up, all had their pew. You always knew where nearly everyone sat. And if visitors came and sat in your pew, you greeted them with unpleasant stares. Once pews left Spring Mount, people likewise could no longer make a claim on pews that had become theirs over the years. The chairs made room for newcomers not to feel they were intruding in someone else's place.

I continued to work part-time after I left the congregation but, as when I left St. Louis, I wondered if I had done the right thing. I had felt so much warmth and acceptance that it was painful to not be a continuing part of Spring Mount.

I have worked at other short-term tasks since. After my third "retirement," I took another interim position as a chaplain at Souderton Mennonite Homes. I commented that I enjoy retiring so much that I took another job so I could retire again.

Chapter 5

The Congregation that Welcomed Only at a Distance: Encountering Racism

AMONG THE PICTURES ON MY STUDY WALL, I always keep a picture of Dr. Martin Luther King, Jr. I recall a memorable morning being in a small group of ministers having breakfast with Dr. King. I sensed I was in the presence of a powerful force for justice. Perhaps it was my imagination that captured me that morning; on the other hand, maybe I sensed I was in the presence of a person whom God chose as a prophet to speak boldly for justice at such a time as that.

I grew up believing that there was no racism in the Mennonite church. I had not read the accounts of systemic racism that existed in some parts of the church. I had not known that in some parts of the church there was a time when people of color could not be greeted with the usual practice of the Holy Kiss when baptized. I soon discovered that marriage between a person of color and a birthright Mennonite was not acceptable. I did not know that all the prejudice that was found in society around us was also alive and well in my own denomination.

My first introduction to racism occurred after a family in our congregation moved back to their hometown in another city. Before their move, three of their girls were in my first baptism class. One of the girls was struck and killed by a train as they were crossing the railroad track. The family chose to take the body to their hometown for burial. I went with them to participate in the funeral, and then it was some time later that the family returned to living in their home town.

There was a Mennonite congregation in that city. I had been told that they had African-American members, so I was pleased that there was a congregation ready to welcome them. And happily, the church was a reasonable driving distance from the family's house. But after attending the church for a few weeks, they began to feel unwelcome. I received a letter from them describing the racism they were experiencing. They finally decided they would no longer attend.

I was puzzled. I knew the congregation had African-American members. What was the trouble? The story I heard later from another source cut deep into my spirit. I learned that a wealthy man in the congregation who contributed heavily to the little struggling congregation insisted that if they let "those people" come, he would withdraw from the congregation. The leaders in the congregation did not have the courage to confront his racist attitude. As a result, the welcome for the two young girls in that family was withdrawn. Still later I learned the African-American members in the congregation were converted in prison and had life sentences. They were members of the congregation but obviously could never attend.

I mused for awhile on what Jesus meant when he talked about offending persons who were young in their faith. Jesus emphasized the gravity of the offense: those who committed such a heinous sin were worthy of having a huge millstone tied around their necks and being cast into the sea.

What is a Christian response when racist persons cut deep wounds into the soul of one they do not understand? If the wounds they inflict cause another to lose faith in God, is there a penalty they must pay? Who ties the millstone around their necks, loads them into a boat, carries them far away from shore, and throws them overboard?

In the case of the wounded family, whom I learned to love and know God loved, my first reaction was that I would have willingly helped tie the stone around the offenders' necks. Perhaps I could have been talked into pushing them overboard, though likely in the process of putting them overboard I would have tipped the boat and fallen in with them.

Jesus used the imagery of the millstone to highlight the magnitude of the sin of offending someone weak in faith. Such sin is not limited to persons of weak faith. It is a sin to discriminate against any person.

There are many ways to hurt and offend other people. Likely the most painful way is to devalue persons because of how they were created by their creator. To say that another's cultural heritage is inferior to our own is to make God a liar. It is to say that God created someone who is bad because that person is not like me. It is to say that God botched things up. It is to declare that God made a mistake when God created someone whose skin is of another color. God then is no longer a God of absolute wisdom and power. God's power becomes limited to a racist's point of view. We then end up saying that the wisdom of the racist is absolute and that God's wisdom is suspect.

Once I traveled with a group of friends from our congregation to another city. I was the only white person among them. We stopped at restaurant for lunch. The restaurant staff told me I could eat but the others in the group could not. Of course I did not eat. My anger over the incident was my lunch that day.

I went to a meeting with a few friends to hear Malcom X address a large gathering of people at a nearby church. When I got to the door, several men firmly informed me that I may not enter. I experienced then a bit of what it must feel like to be denied entrance because of the color of one's skin.

Some might call that racism in reverse. However, I see it as an action by an oppressed group of people to work at their own agenda of seeking justice. There is a significant difference between systemic racism on the part of the powerful European-American population and the powerless African-American people. The racism of a powerful majority is an action, whereas racism of a powerless minority is a reaction. The majority controls the use of power. In the United States, the white majority still controls economic and political power. It is their prerogative to give power to the minority or withhold power. The majority has the power to make laws that benefit those who already have power.

The welfare system over the years, for example, has served well to control a large majority of people. I am not making a case against welfare. Without welfare benefits many people would have been doomed to extreme suffering. When welfare became a tool of the majority to control power over a minority it became, however, part of an evil system.

I recall politicians telling welfare recipients that if they did not vote a certain ticket they would be cut of from welfare. No welfare mother in her right mind would risk losing her check to provide food and housing for her children. The result was that when election day came the corrupt politician was reelected. Votes of the minority persons were welcomed— but not their true voices. Votes of dead people were also welcome. I saw names of persons on the voter registration list for whom I had conducted funerals years earlier. People sometimes likened voting day to the general resurrection: the dead people came back to vote.

Not all politicians are corrupt. Within the welfare system, there are people who care about justice. Some administrators of the system are as powerless as the recipients. Systemic racism is the most subtle and destructive form of racism.

Individual people with racist attitudes have the potential to transform their thinking and seek new understanding of the issues. Their best teachers could be the very ones they discriminate against. Refusing to listen to and get to know persons over whom the racist stands in judgment deepens the scars in the soul. This becomes another bar on the door of the prison racists have constructed for themselves. The people who linger in the cells of their own discrimination and lifestyle of bigotry alone have the key to let themselves out.

Some persons, however, have been blinded to the need to find a key because racism has crept into their life in unsuspected ways. Others enjoy it in their prison cell because they enjoy the sense of power it grants them. Systemic racism values its possessions and power and will go to any lengths not to lose it. Systems bent toward evil do not voluntarily share their power and wealth. The fire hoses and dogs trained to kill during the 1960s were a picture of resistance to sharing power and wealth.

A newly married couple from our congregation spent several years in the armed forces during the Vietnam War. On returning they bought a trailer home in which to begin their life together. Park after park refused to rent space for their trailer. In a few cases I went first to make a contact and there was space available. When the young people appeared and their skin color was not white, there was no longer any space available.

I already felt a deep disdain for our nation's readiness to send some of our best young people to fight in the war. When my friends returned from supposedly "defending their country," the very country they defended would not let them park a trailer in a trailer park because they were not white. Such stories could be multiplied many times over. Things have changed to some degree, but much remains to be changed. Systemic racism is still alive and well.

Perhaps it is a false hope to expect that it will change a great deal. Christians cannot overcome racism until they name it sin. Cardinal Anthony Bevilocqua, Catholic archbishop of Philadelphia, said in excerpts from "Racism Through Faith and Truth," a pastoral letter, that

> How we treat one another cannot be separated from our relationship with God. Unless and until we understand this truth racism and all other sins against our neighbor will remain. Racism is a moral disease and it is contagious. No one is born a racist. Carriers infect others in countless ways, through words, attitudes, deeds and omissions. Yet one thing is certain, the disease of racism can and must be eradicated. We are not born racists we learn it. And what we learn we can unlearn.

If the Cardinal is right that we can unlearn, unlearning becomes a priority. A friend of ours remarked one time that her children were using some racist words. "I never taught them that," she said. Our response was, "What *did* you teach them?" The importance of teaching children positive attitudes about loving all persons created by God cannot be overemphasized. Unlearning is a slow process. It can become painful. It is not easy for some of us to admit that we were wrong. Racist attitudes lodge deeply and securely, hoping not to get disturbed. Perhaps an exorcism formula needs to be prepared to cleanse the demonic evil of racism that can lodge in all of us. Maybe the formula is to open our mind and seek truth. "The truth shall make you free," the Scriptures say.

Our two children were the only white ones in a school of around twenty-five hundred children. It was during the time when the civil rights movement took on a more militant position. One noon Lorna, our daughter, came home for lunch and announced that the "black liberators" were coming that afternoon to kill all the white people. She ate her lunch and skipped off to school, not registering any concern. She obviously felt this did not apply to her. Of course we knew the black liberators would not come. They were not a violent group. Somehow our daughter was able to develop a trust relationship with the children with whom she grew up.

All forms of racism are destructive. Overt racism that is easily detected carries less of a threat then subtle racism that hides behind a facade of piety. The KKK advertised a public meeting to be held in a local park close to where we lived. A friend and I decided to go and see what goes on at a KKK meeting. We went with some trepidation to the meeting place, not sure at all that we should be there or if it was safe. We were greeted at the gate by a large man with a shotgun. We did not let that intimidate us as we proceeded to join about 150 other people at the rally. As we stood listening to the hate speeches, everyone around us looked like us. One could not tell who was a Klan member or who was there for the same reason that took us there.

When the hate speeches were over, the cross-burning ceremony took place. About thirty-five men put on their hoods and robes and formed a circle around the huge cross. Each of the men carried a torch. They all passed in front of the most distinguished man of the Klan, who held a burning torch in his hand. They all set fire to their torch from their elder's torch. As they stood in a circle around the cross, they prayed. The prayer included something about Jesus being the light of the world. It was a prayer one might hear at any gathering of Christian believers. After the prayer, the men walked toward the cross, put their torches against the kerosene-soaked wood, and stood back to watch while flames consumed the cross.

I left that meeting totally disgusted with what I witnessed. But I also left with a valuable lesson. I became aware like never before that it is important that we make clear who we are. I knew exactly who the people were who wore their hoods and robes. I did not know who the people were who stood beside me but did not identify themselves. They might have been people like me. They might have been people who once wore robes. I was not all that concerned about those who wore the robes; their identity was clear. I was concerned about those whose identity was hidden.

The loudmouth racists in our society and institutions are not the real enemies of justice. The real enemies are those within the institution who refuse to identify themselves. They are the people who will not raise their voices when they become aware of racism. They are the people who refuse to let a searchlight focus on their own history to see if subtle racism is going undetected. It is not the "bad" people who create the racial injustice in our society. "Bad" people have only as much power as "good" people allow them to have. When people tell me they are not racists, then I listen a little more intensely to find out what they are covering up. Racism seems to find a harbor in most of us. Paul said he was the "chief of sinners." Perhaps racism is like that in the most of us. The more we grow in awareness of racism, the more we detect it in our own selves.

The roots of racism go back as far as the hatred that developed between Cain and Abel. They did not understand each other or their individual professions. One was a herder of sheep and the other a tiller of the ground. They became jealous of each other and finally one murdered the other. If we have an obsessive need to be better than another, we demonize that person. Demonizing other people legitimizes any hateful action against them. If powerful people sense that their "superior" position is threatened, they have to devise ways to destroy whatever or whoever stands in the way. Murder might even be the most painless way a racist could act against his victims. Even more destructive, in some ways, is hatred leveled against others that devalues them for a lifetime. Murder is as wrong as wrong can be. But if my memory serves me, I recall Jesus said that to hate a person is equal to murder. Racism is a camouflaged form of hatred.

Racism is a cancer among good people. It often goes on for a long time before it is detected. There are people working hard at finding a cure. The Damascus Road project, initiated

Mennonite Central Committee, is an example of an attempt to cure racism. The Damascus Road project works responsibly at training leaders to help congregations and institutions dismantle racism. Progress is slow.

When persons get in touch with their own racism, then their healing can begin. As long as we put on a pious front, denying our own racism, God's healing love can't penetrate the walls of callouses that have so long kept out the light of truth. The prison doors will remain closed. The key is in reach, but prisoners of racism need to do the reaching. Someone can tell them where the key is, but they themselves need to put forth effort to take it from its place, put it into the keyhole, and turn it to open the latch. No one can turn the key for them.

We can tell our story of how we encountered racism. We can share our stories of pain. But as we confront raw racism it always must be in the spirit that Paul spoke to the Galatians, "My friends, if any one is detected in a transgression, you who have received the Spirit should restore such a one in a spirit of gentleness. Take care that you yourselves are not tempted. Bear one another's burdens and in this you will fulfill the law of Christ." (Gal. 6:1, 2)

Chapter 6

Worse than Bullets: Homosexuality and Christian Faith

I AM NOT A THEOLOGIAN WHO HAS EARNED THE RIGHT to speak with authority on the biblical texts regarding faith and homosexuality. I do have more than forty years of ministry experience relating to many disenfranchised people whom society and the church have not always understood or treated fairly. I have participated in developing more then twenty new congregations.

I view congregations as a special gift from God to their communities. In my mind I see a resemblance between the cities of refuge in the Old Testament and today's congregations. The cities of refuge were safe places where the fringe people of society, the offenders, the alienated, and the hopeless, could enter, find acceptance, and rebuild what was taken from them. I long for congregations likewise to become places of safety and centers of hope.

A congregation loses its way when it takes on the nature of a club requiring strict adherence to a code of rules. If the rules are designed only to protect its self-image and limit who may become a member, it is no longer a gift from God to any who have been alienated or have lost their way.

In my use of the cities of refuge concept I do not include the sons and daughters of our own families of faith who were created with same-sex preference. I do not classify them as offenders or people without hope. I include them in the family God loves and uses to bless the world. They already are whole people who minister to those who are not whole. However, the church falls into the trap of treating anyone not created like the majority as an inferior creation.

The most intense challenge I have faced in my many years of ministry has been attempting to work in a redemptive way with the issue of homosexuality. The most painful experience in my ministry was not the bullets sent through my car. It was not looking into the business end of a gun or being beaten unconscious. It was when a congregation I served as overseer was removed from its conference (its regional cluster of congregations), because its members welcomed all persons God brought through its doors.

I recall many meetings with Germantown Mennonite Church and with leaders in Franconia Mennonite Conference. There was pain and there was hope. There was rejection of the congregation by many in the conference because of Germantown's welcome of gays and lesbians. There were also many strong supporters of the congregation whose voices were silenced by louder opposing voices. The congregation needed to live under the searchlight of a conference pressured into removing them from membership.

There was pain because the congregation was asked to not offer membership to those created by God to be attracted to persons of the same sex and to live in a covenantal relationship with another of their gender. There was hope because of voices who made a serious effort to understand and support the congregation and its leaders. There always was a deep sense in the congregation that Jesus is Lord of the church. It is the Lord of the church who welcomes all those who will come to receive God's grace.

One of the more difficult times I experienced was sitting in meetings where good people with a variety of viewpoints attempted to come to a common understanding of faithfulness on this issue. I recall driving home late one evening from a meeting where we seemed to be polarizing. It was hard to separate the theological issues from the political ones. It seemed as though theology was only politics and politics was theology.

In my downcast spirit, I searched for words that would describe the feeling I might have if I were the person discriminated against. What suffering is inflicted on a person whose deepest desire is to serve Christ and the church when told the way God created her or him is sin? I can never know what that feeling is like. I know I could not change who I am as a heterosexual. Persons who are homosexual face a similar impossibility. I can only imagine what pain and disappointment it must be to be told one must change sexual orientation. To be told it was a sin for me to develop a close caring relationship with another same-gender person would grind at my understanding of faith, love, and compassion.

When I got home, I let my imagination run wild for a bit and wrote the following lines. I don't claim inspiration other than that the words were a way to calm my own spirit when I felt hurt over the injustice being meted out against people God loves and I love. I wrote these lines following a painful meeting on Tuesday, September 13, 1994, imagining it was me no longer welcome in the church.

Silent Reflection
Dear God, you do not look on
us as we look on others.
You have love and compassion;
we often stumble into being judgmental,
even when your words say, "Judge not."

We are members of a body
where the ideal is unity.
But there is so much diversity.
We see things from many points of view.
We have a variety of life experiences
and fall into traps
of insisting that we all must think alike.
We judge those who think differently from us.

But God, my standard may not be
the answer that you wish
for all who call on you.
Let me not be bitter
when others do not agree with me.
Thank you for making room for diversity.

But in my journey, God,
I struggle with my anger.
There is so much pain,
when strangers to compassion
rip away the very tenets of my faith.
It feels like a hungry dog
ripping a baby rabbit from its mother's womb.
It's lonely, God,
when no one tries to understand
my journey.

They put on their hunting jackets,
hide behind a clump of trees,
as though I were a deer
in open hunting season,
and shoot at me.
They never talked to me.
They do not know my name.
My beauty they cannot see.
They do not know my mind

or understand my pain.
But they hide behind the bush
and shoot at me.
God, you understand my anger,
do you not?

When the place that once was safe
is turned into a trap,
to catch those whose faith
goes far beyond the faith of those
who set the trap,
I'm angry, God,
with no way to respond.
Angry over the time spent
on matters that tear down
and do not build up.
I'm angry that the friendships formed by time
are being polarized.
I'm angry, God, because
the safety I once knew here
has been invaded—
invaded by my brothers and sisters
who do not know my name.

God, I want to love ones who do not know me.
I want to claim the heritage
that comes from being members
of a family of faith.
I can't help it, God,
that my anger rises so
when my accusers do not know my name.

I'm angry, God,
because of the drain of precious energy
that could have gone to telling of your love.
We could have talked so long

about what we have in common.
We could have gone to feed those
whom you love so much
but who must make the street their home.

I'm angry, God,
because I always thought
our congregation was a special gift from you
to our community.
That vision now is hazy
as though a cloud descended
upon us and blocked out
the brightness of the healing sun.
God, I'm angry
at those who ride that cloud
which hides the sun from us.

An evil thought within me
wants to strike a vicious blow
at those who will refuse to get to know me.
But that would be so wrong.
I then would step down
to the very level
where my accusers stand.
They don't hit with fists,
but if they did,
it would not hurt as much
as being told you have to
abandon precious faith.

God, it hurts so much
when I am told
that you made a big mistake
when you created me.
You know my struggles, Lord,
the many prayers,

the agony,
the pain that pierced my soul
till your peace came to me.

I'm angry, Lord,
because I'm told
that I must enter into that pain again
to try to become
what I can never be.

O GOD, HELP ME!
I cannot hide anything, O God,
from your compassionate eye.
My shortcomings are many. But
my shattered life is becoming whole again,
because you heard my cries
and reached me in my pain.

Forgive me, God.
Many times my faith wandered far away
from what I knew was truth.
My attitudes at times
are kin to my accusers.
God, walk with me in my journey,
if not, I'll go astray.

I now open up myself to you.
Whatever hides in me
that is not true,
remove it with your gentle touch,
and let this part of my journey end.
With you by my side,
I will walk confidently into new beginnings
with courage, hope, and peace
in JESUS CHRIST my Lord.

After I wrote those lines I gained renewed courage to continue seeking God's will in our struggle to find a faithful response to the hard and complex questions that faced us. A committee was appointed by conference to recall the history of the past conversations with the congregation. That committee was made up of persons who sympathetically struggled with the issue and from those who saw the issues through another set of bifocals.

Dialogue continued for over a year. An overseer support committee was appointed to be in conversation with the congregation and bring a proposal to the delegate session of conference for decision-making. The key question was whether the congregation could remain a member of conference if it continued to welcome same-sex persons living in covenantal relationships with each other. The committee worked hard and finally arrived at a statement all of us could support.

The statement went to the conference council. There it was decided that it would not be appropriate to take it to the delegate body. Another proposal was brought instead.

I am usually not the first one to speak out at meetings when the floor is open for discussion. I don't know why I often refuse to trust myself enough to speak out. But in this case I needed to speak. While many were silent I needed to join the few that spoke.

I read a statement earlier that day that made a deep imprint on my mind. The statement said, "If you have truth and it has pain, speak softly." I seldom cry in public but the tears were hard to hold back. I made the following statement, not so much to persuade the body to see things my way but to release in me the pressure that could do me harm. I said, "I constantly need to work at balancing my feelings with the real facts in the issue. Whenever I let my feelings overrule the facts, then I do harm to myself and the issue that concerns me.

"I have worked with the congregation now for more than five years. I have been involved with the congregation in leadership change and in settings of joy and pain. I think I have my feelings tempered with facts, but I also may have been very short-sighted at times. I confess my strong feeling on this issue. I am aware that my position is not acceptable to some people at this meeting. I am also aware that it is a position many others would affirm.

"I have listened to the pain other church bodies have gone through as they have dealt with this issue. I hoped and prayed that our conference could be spared that pain. I am convinced the executive committee worked with integrity to bring this proposal before us today. The congregational and overseer support group also worked with integrity. There were times of sharp disagreement among us. But we prayed together, challenged each other, and sought God's direction together.

"We came to an agreement on a document that we could bring to this conference. We—perhaps I should say I—felt we were led by the Spirit. We all signed the document.

"I have experienced the pain of the congregation and also witnessed their spirit of cooperation. The congregation does not wish to be a burden to the conference. But the congregation values its historic roots and wants to be part of that ongoing stream. They also want to minister to all whom God gives them. I sensed that they want to be a part of all the good gifts God has given the Mennonite church.

"I am deeply hurt that we are at the place of removing a congregation from us because we don't all view the issue from the same perspective. There are many issues we do not affirm with one voice. Our human nature wants us to dig into our pockets for stones, stones we have hidden there for occasions like this, and start throwing them at each other. Unfortunately, I have cast a few stones too.

"Those who are without sin have earned the right to cast the first stone. The rest of us must beg God beg for mercy.

"I have given forty years of my life in ministry to the church I love. It is painful for me to be amid conflict that could seriously fracture the church. In my years of ministry I have experienced pain. I have looked into the business end of a gun. I have been beaten to unconsciousness. I have had bullets come through my car and miss my head by mere inches. I have experienced numerous times of having our house broken into. Yet the pain I feel over a congregation that I love and God loves being removed from conference hurts more than bullets and beatings.

"I have also experienced joy. But the joy is gone for the moment. The pain will likely last awhile. But joy will come back."

At that meeting it was decided not to vote on the issue. At a later time a ballot was mailed to every delegate to vote. It seemed so wrong to me that we needed to vote without the benefit of being together in the same room with brothers and sister to discern what God might be saying to us. I suspect, even though I do not have statistics, that a large majority of the persons who voted to remove Germantown had never talked to anyone in the congregation and likely did not know any of the persons they were standing in judgment over.

That was a gross violation of the Matthew 18 principle Mennonites have honored and valued in the past. My understanding based on Matthew 18 is that if we have an issue with another person, we go to the person first. In this case, leaders who wanted to remove Germantown went to the conference body first. It seemed so ironic to me that an appeal could be made to be faithful to the Scriptures regarding same-sex attraction, even as the very process for doing so turned right around and ignored another Scripture calling for a redemptive process to solve conflict.

The results of the vote by mail strongly supported removing the congregation from conference. On a Tuesday evening, two representatives from the conference shared the vote tally with the congregation. The silence was loud as the sentence was read. It felt like what I once experienced in a courtroom, where the person I had worked with for some time, and of whose innocence I was convinced, was sentenced to death.

The encounter took place in the old historic Germantown meetinghouse. In the cemetery a few yards away lay the body of William Rittenhouse, the first Mennonite minister in North America. More than three hundred years before, he had led the first Mennonites who came from Europe.

A congregation has continued all these years, giving witness of faith and modeling Christian community. Like every congregation I am aware of, Germantown has not always been perfect, but for those of us who value history, it seemed so wrong that at this place a congregation was told it could not be part of the church because its members welcomed whoever God brought their way.

It was also in this congregation that a document was signed protesting the evil of slavery. The table on which that signing took place is is still in the meeting house. One could almost hear the voices of history crying out from the walls and ceiling with groans of disbelief that the congregation which for all these many years proclaimed the gospel could no longer be in formal fellowship with the other Mennonite congregations. Germantown had not experienced anything this painful in all its three centuries.

For me the height of pain occurred when my beloved brother Richard Lichty, the pastor, was told that his credentials would no longer be honored by the conference. Richard had given all his productive years to teaching and preaching. He had chaired important committees in conference. He was loved as a pastor in his former congregation. He had an unusual capacity to interpret Scriptures and had demonstrated appreciation for Anabaptist beliefs. He was a person to whom I would look up and trust. To hear Richard being told that conference no longer would recognize his credentials was like someone putting a big blanket over the sun and hiding the light.

On that Tuesday evening, an appropriate response to the outcome of the delegate vote did not surface. It felt as though one should scream, cry, and laugh at the same time. Silence seemed to work best.

The pain was felt not only by the congregation. I suspect that when the conference representatives write their story, they will also talk about the anguish they experienced in carrying out the wishes of the larger body. My finger is not pointing at those two people who conveyed our "sentence," even though I wish we could have found within ourselves the gift of arriving at a common mind.

Hurt people at that meeting expressed their pain and anger at what had happened. One Germantown participant asked to be symbolically ushered out of the meeting place. Because he was gay, he said, he had faced many rejections.

With a great deal of hesitation, making it clear it was not the personal wish of that conference official but the act of a conference representative, the official escorted him out the door. The pastor made a similar request. Surrounded by pain, he too was escorted out of the meetinghouse as a symbol of the congregation's removal from conference.

Never had I experienced such high drama as I witnessed that evening. I felt that sin had lifted its most ugly face. It was not the sins of the congregation or any people in the congregation or the sins of the conference representatives. It seemed to me to be the sins of a system wrapped in piety and blind to compassion that made two of its leaders carry out the "guilty" verdict.

After the anger and the crying subsided, someone suggested that we sing. The hymn books were brought out. The walls of the historic 1770 meetinghouse must still echo the refrain from that beautiful song, "My Life Flows On":

> My life flows on in endless song,
> above earth's lamentation.
> I catch the sweet, though far off hymn

that hails a new creation.
No storm can shake my inmost calm
while on the rock I'm clinging.
Since love is Lord of heaven and earth,
how can I keep from singing?
Through all the tumult and the strife,
I hear the music ringing.
It finds an echo in my soul.
How can I keep from singing?
What though my joys and comforts die?
The Lord my Savior liveth.
What though the darkness gather round?
Songs in the night he giveth.
The peace of Christ makes fresh my heart,
a fountain ever springing!
All things are mine since I am his!
How can I keep from singing?
(*Hymnal: A Worship Book*, 580)

That refrain will always be riveted in my mind and heart. It was that song God used to start the healing for me. I may hold the record of being the person most incapable of carrying a tune, but "how can I keep from singing." I think God used that hymn to point out to me that God is so present in our pain. In fact when we feel a little pain, God feels greater pain. God cares more about a congregation and its people, wounded as they may be, than we could ever care. I do hope at my funeral the people gathered for celebration will lift their voices and sing joyously, "My life flows on."

I have talked mostly about my feelings and have not yet addressed the issue of how I understand—or perhaps do not understand—homosexuality and faith. We have a vision statement accepted by our denomination that calls for healing and hope. Included in the statement are the following directives: "God calls us to be followers of Jesus Christ, and, by the power of the Holy Spirit, to grow into communities of grace, joy, and peace, so that God's healing and hope flow through us to the world."

Healing and hope will not come as long as we disenfranchise congregations before we have exercised patience, time, and discernment to discover how God is leading us. For healing and hope to permeate our church will require growth in our ability to exercise patience and love toward each other. Healing and hope demand that we understand persons we would criticize as fully as we can. To understand others is not to talk about them but to talk with them. The more we talk with one whom we do not understand the more our need to judge subsides. The more we talk with others, the more we are enabled also to walk with them. It is in walking with others that we can enter their joy and pain.

I could not understand what the hurry was to take this action with Germantown. I understand that in biblical history there was a period of four hundred years when there was no word from the Lord. I wonder how different the outcome would have been if we would have covenanted together to lay the issue down for only ten years. That would have been a short time compared to four hundred. There were voices in the conference who said we could wait no longer to take action. So we took action. We have not yet arrived at the tollgate for the action we took. In reality, I think we freed the congregation to be what God called its people to be and bound the conference, preventing its being what it could be until some deep soul-searching takes place.

I am addressing the issue of homosexuality and faith from a pastor/mentor viewpoint. I am basically limited to asking questions. Perhaps the questions are more important than the answers. At least it is never safe to give answers when we do not understand the question. I am not sure I am always asking the right questions. But they are the questions that concern me. They are the questions for me at this time. For me the quest is for faithfulness in extending the great invitation to all people to become participants in Christ's kingdom and members of a local congregation. Who then do we exclude or include?

The church is on a journey, growing in awareness of having the mind of Christ as we address faith and homosexuality. And the issue is a complex one. One can almost be certain that a simple easy answer for a complex question is the wrong one. Sometimes there isn't any answer, and we are forced to live with some ambiguity.

It has been relatively easy for us who are Mennonites to make major shifts in the practice of our faith. The more we have identified with our society, the easier it has become to adapt to new understandings and practices in relation to convictions we once held dear and sacred. We laid aside our biblical interpretation of 1 Corinthians 11 and no longer hold head covering for women to be a test of membership.

The more we become acculturated, the easier it becomes to change theology. It is not easy instead to make changes that move counter to the prevailing mood of society. There seems to be a popular conservative religious ship in the river of our society that carries a banner condemning all homosexuality as evil and we find it difficult indeed to do otherwise.

There seems to be little or no attempt to try to understand the fact that for some people there is no choice. Not all people for whom there is no choice are evil. There are evil choices made by both heterosexuals and homosexuals. To condemn a whole group of people because a few in the group make bad choices would mean that both heterosexuality and homosexuality are evil. No one is wise enough to condemn another, especially when the fruit of the Spirit is evident in the one we wish to condemn.

Considering the amount of attention homosexuality is getting in the church, I am surprised that the Bible does not speak out in greater volume. Are the Scriptures clear enough to call for judgment on all gays and lesbians who live in a covenantal relationship? The claim is made that the issues of slavery and the role of women in leadership can be argued both ways from the Scripture. Regarding homosexuality, that claim cannot be made. Might it be that one cannot argue both ways from the Scripture on homosexuality because on close examination the Bible is silent about committed Christians who are gay or lesbian and live in a covenantal relationship? The Bible does address immorality by heterosexuals and homosexuals.

Of course I can imagine an argument to the effect that gays and lesbians in a covenantal relationship are not Christians, so the Bible has nothing to say about their situation. But Jesus also does not say anything about homosexuality. This does not mean it was not an issue then but does suggest it was not a hot-button issue like it is today. Jesus did address some hot-button issues; the result was his rejection and crucifixion. It is some of those destructive sins Jesus addressed that we refuse to take seriously. Sins of greed, of abuse of wealth and power, and of devaluing people whom God created were the ones Jesus hit hard.

As I will soon explore, the Leviticus laws draw attention to homosexuality, as do several New Testament passages. Meanwhile the Sodom and Gomorrah story is often understood as portraying the evils of same-sex genital activity. The story records that every man in the city, young and old, mobbed the house of Lot and demanded that his two visitors be brought out to them for a wicked act. Lot's offering of his daughters complicates the story more.

Could one make a case that for Lot to offer his daughters for the sexual gratification of the men at the gate would have been acceptable? Common sense and moral dignity tells us this would be wrong. The story of Sodom portrays immorality in it worst form. It tells of fallen humanity and the depth of depravity to which humans are capable of descending.

The angels that came to warn Lot to take his family out of the city because it was going to be destroyed had their message from God before this one infamous scene took place. The city was going to be destroyed because its citizens were awash in selfish indulgence in pleasure. Ezekiel wrote what the real sin of Sodom was: "This was the guilt of your sister Sodom; she and her daughters had pride, excess of food, and prosperous ease, but did not aid the poor and needy" (Ezek. 16: 49).

There is no question that the story contains sexual immorality. But the root of Sodom's sin, according to Ezekiel, had to do with pride, excess of food, and prosperous ease. Perhaps the problem that brings judgment on our church is not homosexuality but our prosperity, excess of food, and not aiding the poor. Jesus does not pick up the theme of homosexuality but does address at length the dangers of wealth. The issue most able to destroy our church is not how we handle homosexuality but how we deal with wealth.

In Matthew 10:5-15 Jesus instructed the disciples to gather in the lost sheep of the house of Israel. The way to do that was to proclaim good news and cure the sick. He told them, "You received without payment; give without payment." He suggested that the gospel of the kingdom cannot be bought. Jesus told them to leave the city if the people would not welcome them. Those who rejected the good news would experience judgment greater than the judgment of Sodom. As Sodom was destroyed for not welcoming the stranger, so would be judged those who did not welcome the stranger bearing the good news.

I wonder why Jesus drew on economics ("You received without payment. . . .") at the same time as he used the Sodom illustration. In addition to Jesus' strong linkage of the destruction of Sodom with not receiving the stranger, there are hints here of concern that Sodom's sin included economic privileges whose fruits the people of Sodom spent on their own voracious appetites.

Whatever Jesus specifically intended, he makes no mention of homosexuality, which fits with the conclusion that the

Sodom story is not primarily about homosexuality but about the sin of abusing the power economic privilege gives. Wealth can shut out the needs and cries of the needy and oppressed.

Jesus sent out the disciples as "sheep amid wolves." I wonder if the wolves are the self-righteous people who stand in judgment of all who do not think or believe like they do. If so, Jesus was saying—and this is certainly borne out in his many other condemnations of those who wrongly congratulate themselves—that self-righteous people stand in greater judgment than do even the sinners of Sodom.

In Matthew 11 there is an account of Jesus proclaiming the message of the kingdom in the cities. He pronounced woes on them. The woes were a result of the blindness and inability to see the power of God at work. If Sodom, Jesus said, would have had the demonstrations of God's grace and love and power as these cities had, Sodom would not have been destroyed. We have seen God's demonstration of power and love. If we make the sin of Sodom homosexuality instead of abuse of wealth and power and withholding from the needy, then maybe we stand in judgment even greater than Sodom's.

Perhaps I have made too much of wealth. Perhaps I have made too little of it. Or perhaps I have only made a small scratch on the surface of an issue the church is not ready to face. Dealing with homosexuality does not take away our need to address our economic privileges. Jesus taught that "It is easier for a camel to go through the eye of a needle than for someone who is rich to enter the kingdom of God" (Mark 10:25). "But woe to you who are rich, for you have received your consolation" (Luke 6:24). Perhaps making homosexuality such a hot-button issue is a version of straining out a little gnat so we can swallow the big economic camel without getting an upset stomach.

In light of this, it is interesting that, to the best of my knowledge, we have cast out congregations over the gnat but not over the camel of wealth or other moral lapses the New

Testament highlights. So should rich people not be part of the kingdom and of the body of Christ, the church? If we treated the wealth passages the same as we sometimes do Paul's statements on homosexuality, we would need to cast all rich people from the church. We would need to remove any congregation from conference which has members who are rich.

Can we safely draw an analogy between the issue of homosexuality in the church and riches? There are many more explicit warnings in the Scriptures over wealth than there are over homosexuality. Or are those questions one does not ask? The prophets declared judgment on individuals and nations that oppress the poor. Nations fell because of abuse of power. Wealth is power. Those who receive an invitation to the "marriage supper of the lamb" are those who have on fine linen robes, bright and pure, "for the fine linen is the righteous deeds of the saints" (Rev. 19:8). The righteous deeds of the saints include caring for all who are marginalized by our society. It is a grievous sin to devalue any of God's children. Jesus said that to do so puts the offender in danger of a hell of fire.

There are rich people in the church whose gifts I value. The fruit of the Spirit is evident in their lives. They care about the spiritual needs of their friends and of alienated people in the world. Their commitment to Christ is without question. Why would we want to remove them from our fellowship? Not all rich people are Christians. Does that mean that no rich people are Christians? Since many homosexuals are not Christian, does that mean that no homosexuals are Christians?

Then of course there still are the Leviticus texts. When Leviticus 18:22 says, "You shall not lie with a male as with a women; it is an abomination," that seems clear and to the point. But what do we do with the many other Leviticus laws to which we pay no attention? Do we isolate and choose at will which are to be obeyed and which ignored? Should we adhere strictly to the law of not wearing garments made of different kinds of cloth? If so, we may not wear garments that are part cotton and part nylon. Our best crops on the farm, when I was a boy, came from the fields that had a mixture of barley and oats.

When the Leviticus codes were written, there was likely little understanding that a small minority of people were not heterosexual. The Leviticus code dealt with heterosexual persons who engaged in unnatural sex acts. For same-sex oriented persons who have not chosen their orientation, the application is very different from heterosexual persons who "unnaturally" engage in same-sex activity.

There is mounting evidence in Scripture and in our society that sexual sins, be they heterosexual or homosexual, are "an abomination unto the Lord." Sexuality is a special gift from God. To abuse any gift God gives brings judgment; that is the key principle to be applied.

In 1 Corinthians Paul identifies a number of kinds of persons who are not candidates for membership in Christ's kingdom. Sodomites are included. Are the Sodomites homosexuals? Or are they greedy people who will not welcome strangers and give to the needy? There are lists in Galatians 5:19-21 and 1 Corinthians 5:11 in which Paul does not include homosexuality. Romans 1:26-27 is the only reference in the New Testament which gives as much as one complete sentence on same-sex intercourse.

Paul does not specifically clarify his reason for opposing same-sex intercourse. Was he referring to adult males who exploited young boys for sexual pleasure? Is the issue prostitution regardless of gender? It was not uncommon for a master sexually to abuse his male slaves. Perhaps Paul is referring to homoerotic acts found among the Gentiles. Paul gives little indication of understanding that some people were created with a fundamental orientation toward same-sex attraction.

Suppose we closely examine those of Paul's passages frequently used to cast out people. Do they include those who are gay or lesbian who have dedicated their lives to Christ and the church? Does Paul talk about the sons and daughters in our faith communities who are gay and who serve Christ faithfully? Or is he talking about people who have turned their back on God? In Romans 1:21-27 Paul says that

> though they knew God, they did not honor him as God or give thanks to him, but they became futile in their thinking, and their senseless minds where darkened. Claiming to be wise, they became fools; and they exchanged the glory of the immortal God for images resembling a mortal human being or birds or four-footed animals or reptiles. Therefore God gave them up in the lusts of their hearts to impurity, to the degrading of their bodies among themselves, because they exchanged the truth about God for a lie and worshiped and served the creature rather then the Creator, who is blessed forever! Amen. For this reason God gave them up to degrading passions. Their women exchanged natural intercourse for unnatural, and in the same way also the men, giving up natural intercourse with women, were consumed with passion for one another.

I do not identify in this passage the sincerely and deeply committed Christians who are gay and lesbian with whom I have had opportunity to counsel. Paul seems unlikely to have had in mind persons who knew already at a very early age that they were different than most others of their age group.

It is important to read the entire list of sins Paul describes in Romans 1. The list contains envy, murder, strife, deceit, gossip, slander; those who are God-haters, insolent, haughty, boastful, inventors of evil, rebellious toward parents, foolish, heartless, and ruthless. These sins and sinners deserve the penalty of death. Who of us would be alive if the death penalty were meted out in relation to these sins?

I am not advocating that we take a soft position on sin. I am suggesting that we not pick out a sin of our own choosing and elevate it over other sins to avoid those in which we are most implicated. Are we, for instance, sometimes involved in the sin of heartlessness even as we home in homosexual sexual expression as the one practice we want to be the cause for casting persons out of the community? We need much more grace and wisdom and the power from the Holy Spirit to discern what God is saying to us.

As long as ethnic heritage held Mennonites together, we did not have to face some of the issues we must confront today. Since we are becoming a multi-ethnic church we need to work through a new set of questions. To take a hardline position which discriminates against believers who are gay and lesbian, who bear the fruit of the Spirit, will close the possibility for us to build Anabaptist-Mennonite congregations in the city or in the country for that matter. We will instead need to develop congregations that limit themselves to simple and definitive answers, whether or not they fit life's complexities.

In my years of ministry in the city, I became convinced that the future of our church is in the city. Our theology of peace and justice made sense to me there in the city, the arena where people were struggling for dignity and equal opportunity. I saw that with casting out Germantown, we were casting out an open door for sharing our faith in the city.

I am still on a journey in my thinking about many issues. I am ready to carve on stone that it is a sin to discriminate against any persons for how they were created by God. Yet I will not live long or wisely enough to carve all my conclusions regarding complex issues on stone. So I write this on "paper" as a declaration of where I am in my understanding now.

I am willing risk asking questions but not wise enough to know what all the questions are. We are always taking risks in living out our faithfulness to Christ. We take risks when we ask questions for which we have no easy answers. We take risks when we try to understand another's point of view. We take risks when we declare firmly where we stand. We take risks when we try to live out what our conscience tells us.

The greatest risk we will ever take is when we decide to follow Jesus and be a disciple. As we follow Jesus, we need to remember that there is an overarching mandate in Scripture not to devalue anything or anyone God created. Peter's vision taught him not to call unclean anything that God has cleansed. Gentiles were acceptable to God to become candidates for kingdom membership. They were not asked to conform to all Jewish tradition.

Choosing faith is a choice. Regardless of sexual orientation, everyone is called on to make a choice to follow Christ. The choice also includes the freedom to take the good that God made and turn it into evil. The honey bee and the hermit spider both distill nectar. The bee makes it into sweet honey. The spider makes it into the most deadly poison know to humankind. Human beings can take what God has given them and make it into something sweet or turn it into poison.

In light of our ability to make something nurturing or poisonous from the Scriptures and lives God gives us, I find it necessary to walk cautiously when it comes to giving concrete answers. Answers that discriminate against anyone who has been created by God are not answers I can accept. I need to listen to my brothers and sister who are gay to ask the right questions. I also need to remain aware of what new scientific information becomes available. As trusted biblical scholars open the Scripture for me, I may need to make some shifts in my understanding of what the Creator is all about in God's world. I will also need to listen to the different views of my brothers and sisters in the church.

As we listen to each other's different stances, is there room for diversity among us? Are there ever times we can change our minds on an issue? In Mennonite history there was once strong emphasis on uniformity in dress. There may have been valid reasons for advocating such a position, even though there are no biblical texts that unambiguously support it. If indeed there were such texts, we would likely see them now—when emphasis on uniform dress has faded—as having been taken out of context during that former era.

Mennonites struggled through the 1 Corinthians 11 text concerning head coverings for women. More recently most Mennonites have experienced freedom of conscience not to insist that women wear a covering. We accept into full membership those who do not see 1 Corinthians 11 and our historic interpretation of that Scripture as a binding rule.

Not so long ago, Mennonites and many other Christian denominations held that divorced persons could not be members of the church. There are biblical texts to support such a position. Jesus spoke rather directly about divorce. Yet I am convinced that the Holy Spirit guided the church in dealing redemptively with divorced and remarried people as it moved toward a more grace-oriented position while not minimizing the gravity of divorce. I only hope we will listen to the Spirit again in relation to same-sex orientation.

Another teaching that sheds light on our ability to change our minds regarding interpretation of Scripture is our reading of 1 Corinthians 14:34 and 1 Timothy 2:8-15. At first reading, it seems clear women should not be in congregational leadership roles. Was my participation in ordaining women for leadership in a congregation a violation of Scripture?

In recent history the Mennonite church, again along with many others, took a strong position against ordination of women. Many congregations still will not accept a woman as pastor. Somehow we have managed to live together in the same conference with widely differing views on women in leadership. I do not anticipate that the church will divide over the variety of positions congregations hold; it looks as though we will be able to live together with that diversity in our midst.

The question of homosexuality places us in a new arena. It stretches us almost to the breaking point. Indeed it will break us if we work carelessly or dishonestly at finding our direction. My question again has to do with how we read the Bible. For some the question has very clear answers. "The Bible says it, I believe it, and that settles it." For others it is not clear at all. Some can live with less clarity, while others need definitive answers.

The reality is that we are a long way from being of one mind. Can we experience God's grace and love and respond to God in obedience when we are not of the same mind? Could we make an honest effort to arrive at least at achieving the same mind to accept those who are of a different mind?

God has had patience with all of us for a long time. God's patience continues. If it did not, then we all would be in serious trouble. So an honest search for a direction from God must go on.

To be faithful to God also requires one to be faithful to oneself. To be faithful to our own self may sometimes place us in a lonely minority position. Not to obey conscience can destroy faith and inflict psychological harm. If we can find a way to allow the Holy Spirit to guide us, then we can praise God even though we hold firmly and with deep conviction to diverse views.

Chapter 7

"They Won't Let Me Cry": Becoming a Caring Congregation

DURING A DISCUSSION PERIOD AFTER I SPOKE about my understanding of the church being a very special gift from God to a broken and fragmented world, conversation took place over the perceived inability to curb the direction our society is heading.

Someone asked, "What do you think the world will look like twenty years from now?"

My simple, hopefully not simplistic, answer was, "What the world will look like twenty years from now will depend on what the church looks like twenty years from now."

Is there enough salt left to preserve the world? Where will the light come from to enable people to read the road signs and make the right turns at the intersections of life?

I value my teachers who taught me about theology and the church. One of those teachers was an eight-year-old girl. While I was camp pastor, the little girl was referred to me by her counselor. The girl had never been away from home before. She was homesick and wanted her mother.

The counselor came to me and said, "We can't stop her from crying; would you talk to her?"

I agreed. So Jane and I sat on a log under the shade of a big maple tree. She had a lot of pain inside her. She was away from her mother for the first time. The surroundings were all new to her. The woods and country were very different from the city that had been home all her eight years. Her old friends were not close by. The sun did not seem to shine through the heavily wooded forest. Jane was afraid and needed to cry.

As we sat on the log she began to sob and said, "They won't let me cry." Streams of tears were watering the log we sat on. "I just want to cry and they won't let me cry," she said again. "Nobody listens when I cry."

I assured her that it was okay to cry and I would stay right with her while she cried. I also tried to assure her that we loved her very much and that her mother loved her even more.

After the reservoir of tears began to dry up and the pace of the sobs slowed, I saw a little smile break through. With her blue eyes still moist with tears, but with a new twinkle, she looked into my eyes and said, "Is it okay for me to hug you now?"

Of course it was okay! I assured her I would be available whenever she needed to cry. Jane skipped off to play games with the other children. I remained under the maple tree for awhile. I reflected on the little counseling session. Not what I taught Jane but what Jane taught me. Two statements Jane made kept making a deep impression in my mind. One was, "They won't let me cry"; the other was, "Is it okay for me to hug you now?"

Jane taught me something about the church my professors had not been able to get me to understand. She taught me that the church is there to listen and be with people when they need to cry. And after the crying is over, the church must receive the hugs that come from wounded people. So often we think that our mission is to stop people from crying. And when the crying is over, we are afraid to get close enough to receive their hugs.

I was invited to a banquet attended by about sixty developmentally disabled persons and volunteers who befriended them. The tone of the banquet was set by the hugs they gave each other. I have rarely witnessed the friendliness I saw there. Their laughter was from their heart. No one was a stranger. Their unpretentious nature was expressed in their "thank you" speeches. Their prayers were simple but profound. The songs they sang had depth of meaning even though not always on key. As I entered into the spirit of that gathering, I became convinced that here surely must be the place where God's image was reflected in its purest form.

I have also attended meetings of theologians and church bureaucrats. Sometimes those meetings became gymnastic exercises to prove who held a right theology and who was in error. Instead of gentle pats on the back, the shoe on the lower part of the anatomy might be more descriptive. Meetings where bureaucrats and theologians gather sometimes become more like a football game. The plays have been well rehearsed. The players are well prepared and the goal is not to come away a loser. If you have to inflict pain on another to win, that is a small price to pay for the trophy.

For theologians to help shape the good news and keep it good, they too need to learn to give hugs, say "Thank you," reach out for friendship, sing off-key, and laugh at themselves. Defining Christ's church must be done hand-in-hand with the developmentally disabled and the well-trained theologian. The wounded and the healers together need to share in the discernment task. The affluent and the poor must have an equal voice. The educated and the uneducated must sit side by side. The lawyer and the farmer and the trash collector need to be in the circle. The voice and the wisdom of both the heart surgeon and the sewer cleaner need to be heard. The preacher's and the janitor's wisdom must equally be accepted. Theology must be discerned and agreed upon on a level playing field where every voice is important and heard from.

It is in the church that all people are our brothers and sisters. No one is better or worse then another. An ancient rabbi once asked his pupils how they could tell when night had ended and the day was on the way back.

"Could it be," asked one student, "when you can see an animal in the distance and tell whether it is a dog or a sheep?"

"No," answered the rabbi.

"Could it be," asked another, "when you can look at a tree and tell whether it is a fig or a peach tree?"

"No," said the rabbi.

"Well then when is it?" his pupils demanded.

"It is when you look on the face of any woman or man and see that she or he is your sister or brother. Because if you cannot do this, then no matter what time it is, it is still night."

The church is a community of people who have accepted the invitation to embody the reality of the presence of the living God. In Jesus Christ, God became flesh and entered into all that makes us human. God's presence and power light every darkened crevice of the human experience. The Holy Spirit is the enabler from whom comes the power to live out God's purpose for humankind.

As God has revealed his will, word, ways, and presence through Jesus, so he continues to use the church to live out God's intentions. The church's mandate is to be faithful in allowing God's presence to infiltrate every aspect of human society. The final authority of the church is the fundamental teachings of Jesus as he taught with words, actions, and deeds as well as silence.

God's authority over the church demonstrated by his presence in the church frees the church to become reconciling agents of God. The church invites all people to experience God's presence. The church is never removed far enough from its human character to make it totally free from error, but the gift of the Holy Spirit guides the members of the church in discerning, fallibly but meaningfully, God's truth. The process of discerning truth also requires confession and repentance. There never is room to put on an ostentatious act of piety to prove righteousness, which is best demonstrated by working for justice for oppressed people.

The church gatherings are like an orchestra. The members of the church come together to fine-tune each instrument for high quality performance. The church must never allow structures, systems, political movements, power institutions, or persons with selfish motives to dictate the church's course of action. If beholden to self-interest, institutions lose the prophetic instruments of the orchestra. The church's song must always involve standing against any evil that hinders God's freeing acts of grace. The church's prophetic stance in the face of evil and injustice may cause suffering; it cost Jesus his life. When the church is faithful even to the point of suffering, however, the very gates of hell cannot prevent its music from conveying God's presence in a secular society.

A broken people can most effectively be God's reconciling agents in the world. God's plan for salvation was not complete before Jesus was broken on the cross and restored through the resurrection. The memorial service around the communion table symbolizes broken people being restored to wholeness. The restoration is a gift to us that comes from the fact that Jesus was broken. The bread is broken and the grapes are crushed so that out of crushing and breaking springs new life.

I am aware of congregations wounded through no fault of their own. I am also aware of some that created their own wounds. Yet whatever the cause, whenever the broken pieces come together again, then the church becomes more what God intended it to be. Sometimes light and salt do not flow out of a congregation until it is broken.

There always is pain when there is conflict and division in a congregation. I have walked with a number of congregations going through pain. Seeing tears flow among disappointed people who care deeply about their church is a sign of hope.

Caring enough to cry is the beginning of a journey toward wholeness.

A congregation that has no conflict likely has little life and vitality. Not that conflict is good, but conflict can arise when there is an effort to be good. Whenever there is a process in the congregation to discern truth, the potential for conflict rises close to the surface. Not everyone is of the same mind. The variety of experiences that come through training, tradition, and vocations among participants in a congregation give many different lenses to view the issue at hand. Some people are always persistent that their position is the right one. Some have the capacity to be more skilled communicators, which can be interpreted as an unfair advantage. Then there are some who have carefully studied the issue and can speak with authority.

Out of such a mix, truth for this time is discerned. What is accepted as truth might be modified somewhere along the way as new information arises. Truth that can be trusted comes when a broken people in honesty and sincerity open themselves up to hear what God may be saying.

When the broken pieces are put back together again, some scars will likely remain. With the proper glue, the pieces glued back together are often stronger at that joint than they were before the break. If the whole were to break again, it likely would not do so at the same line that was previously broken. The glue that binds the broken together is the forgiveness, compassion, and love experienced in a community of faith.

As a younger man, I recall hearing many sermons that laid sin bare for all to see and judge but never held a light to show the way to forgiveness. The road to God was so narrow and the ditch along the side was so deep that if one fell in, there were few ways to get back out. No one was trained to rescue those who fell. Leaders understood their role as that of law enforcement agents and judges. Justice was understood as measuring out punishment for disobedience to the rules. It was much later in life that I heard sermons from the gospel and the words of Jesus that call his followers to work for justice, let the oppressed go free, and preach good news to the poor.

Jesus made a visit to the house of Simon, who was a leper. Among the dinner guests was a woman with an alabaster jar of expensive ointment. As they sat at the table, she poured this expensive ointment on Jesus' head.

The disciples became irritated at what they believed was a waste of money. "This ointment could have been sold for a large sum and the money given to the poor," they said. Jesus replied, "Why do you trouble this women? She has performed a good service for me." Jesus told them they would always have the poor with them.

I have heard some interpret that Matthew 26 passage as saying God predestined some people to be poor. What Jesus was actually telling them, I believe, was that their ministry would be to poor people. Poor people would always be close by, but he would not be. Perhaps they had forgotten that Jesus said his call from God was to "preach good news to the poor."

It is in faithful congregations that the poor are valued and the good news is preached to them. The good news is also a loaf of bread when someone is hungry. Good news is an opportunity to be gainfully employed. Good new is to be welcomed into the educational system. Good news is to be able to participate in and benefit from systems designed for all people. I often liken the system of social justice to subway transportation systems. Once you have a token to get in, you can ride all day if you wish. The token gives the rider that privilege. The poor have no tokens to get into the system. The church should be a voice calling for no one to be denied a token.

Good news is hearing a word from someone who loves you and tells you God loves you. Proclaiming the good news among poor people is a holy call from God. Every person needs to hear good news, but Jesus seemed to single out the poor as the ones to hear it first. The lowly shepherds were the first to hear the announcement that the bearer of the best news known to humankind was born.

There is no intrinsic virtue in being poor. Rich and poor people alike will be called on to give an account for their personal response to the good news. Being poor is no excuse for unfaithfulness. The poor stand ahead of the line to hear the good news. "The first shall be last, and the last shall be first," Jesus said one time.

So I need to come back again to the question, "What will the world look like in twenty years?" If the church can recapture its call to do justice, the world will be a very different place. But if the church can no longer hear the prophets among the people, then the salt and light will erode away like topsoil flowing into the river after a heavy rain. If it keeps eroding, eventually there will be no fertile soil left in which to plant seeds of justice and from which to harvest the fruit of peace. Justice will remain a stranger to those for whom there is no justice now.

If there is no longer a voice calling into question the insanity of war, nations will be consumed by their building of weapons. If the church does not value those civilian lives a nation may be all too ready to sacrifice in its pursuit of terrorists, who will? If the church will not give leadership regarding environmental concerns, who will? If the church supports capital punishment, who will tell the state about the folly of murdering a person to prove that murder is wrong?

When the church no longer cares about justice for all people, it gives itself a license to exclude anyone its members do not understand or like. Racism can then be justified and homophobia welcomed. The Scriptures can be used to support the vilest of sins and condemn what does not fit an acceptable mode. The Bible can be used to make "murderers," people who kill for the state, acceptable members of a congregation. It can be used to support slavery. It can be used to make sinners out of people whose ways the church dislikes. A proof text can be found to reinforce almost any heresy.

The church that cares about justice for all people is the real light and salt of the earth. God will not forever stand by and watch members of his creation crush other members. If the prophets do not cry out, then God will choose another way. When Jesus made his triumphal entry into Jerusalem, a multitude of followers began to praise God joyfully and with a loud voice. Some of the religious leaders in the crowd asked Jesus to order his disciples to stop their praises and shouts. To this Jesus replied, "I tell you, if these were silent, the stones would shout out" (Luke 19:40).

If today the church remains silent and does not step into the gaps of injustice, God will call out the stones and their voices will be heard. I'm not wise enough to know who the stones are God will use, but God chooses the most unlikely people to bring about God's will on earth. Throughout history God has always used the most unlikely people for kingdom work. In the genealogy of Jesus, Matthew names some of the most unlikely people to pass their genes on to the Messiah. There was Tamar, a prostitute. There was Rahab,who also was a prostitute and had provided for the safety of the spies. Then there was Ruth the Moabite, who by Jewish standards should not have been included in the genealogy of Jesus.

What a shame if the church stands by and does not even notice when God is doing a new thing. It is sad that good people out of their blindness condemn what God is doing in bringing about God's will "on earth as it is in heaven." How tragic it is when the church comes to Jesus to ask him to silence the voices that shout praises of joy or to ask those who work for justice for the oppressed to stop.

But I have hope. The gates of hell cannot prevent the church from being what God wants it to be. The church in the future may look very different from the church we know and love now. The church that God can use is a church that will conform to God's will. It will refuse to be formed by a society that no longer cares about justice. The church God will use is a church with the ability to change as times call for change. That church will accept new insight God provides. It will dig its roots deep into God's grace, love, and compassion. It will learn to drink so deeply from the fountain of God's justice that justice will flow out from it as an ever-flowing stream.

Whenever there are sharp disagreements in a congregation over matters of theology and doctrine there is potential for division. The Christian church is riddled with division. When parties involved in debate try to outdo each other, both lose. If they try to outdo each other in love and compassion, then both win. I have heard many arguments over a correct interpretation of theology. Almost in every case it was, in the final analysis, a struggle for control and power. An honest search for truth seldom leads to division. There may be times when relations grow strained, but with proper attitudes of love and honest attempts to see the other's point of view, growth will result.

How peaceful our world could be if only the church would practice its own beliefs. If the church only practiced its own creed, which calls for loving the neighbor as one's own self, what a difference it would make in the world. If the golden rule could be understood to imitate God's love rather than being interpreted as "They that have the gold make the rules," justice could again rule. Our congregations can become classrooms in which we learn about and teach how to love the world as God loves the world. A faithful church that practices justice for all will leave a kinder and friendlier world for the next generation.

Chapter 8

"You Are that Man": The Church, Political Structures, and Mission

*T*HERE IS A ROLE FOR THE PROPHET in the church. The prophet cries out warnings when justice is denied. When the "weak" prophet confronts a "powerful" institution, there is good reason indeed for fear and trembling. Nathan the prophet must have retained extraordinary courage to confront the powerful King David over the sins David had committed with Bathsheba and against Bathsheba's husband. Nathan's fear to confront David was overcome by his deep sense that he was called by God to speak against the injustice committed by the king.

Despite Nathan's call from God, however, he must have experienced anxiety. Who was he to call into question the king? The king was great and powerful and did many good things. It would have been easier for Nathan to let this one slip by. It was likely not politically expedient to make this act of the king an issue while the king was waging a war; people who question a king at a time like that are often viewed as traitors. David's good outweighed the bad, so why call him on this?

Not to mention the fact that David had the power to support or destroy Nathan's role as a prophet.

With David's goodwill, Nathan could have become a distinguished political leader. He could have entered into a power play with David so both of them could win. He could have gone to David and said, "Look David, it was not right for you to do these immoral acts. If this leaks to the press, you will do yourself and the people much harm. As God's prophet, I really should speak out against your grievous sin. But let me suggest this, David: being a prophet is a lonely job. People hate us. There is so much good we prophets can do. If we had a little support from you, our task would be much easier. After all, we all sin a little."

Nathan as true servant of God refused to play any such political games. He needed no king to do him a favor. He refused the power and prestige he could have had by mellowing his approach and rationalizing away the gravity of the issue. Nathan refused to become entangled in any political and institutional structure that took away from him the authority to cry out, "Thus says the Lord."

If Nathan had not exercised his authority as a prophet from God, David might never have repented of his sin. Although scholars debate to what extent David was author of such a psalm, David's true sorrow and remorse for his sin may well be expressed in the lines in Psalm 51:

> Have mercy on me, O God,
>   according to your steadfast love;
> according to your abundant mercy
>   blot out my transgressions.
> Wash me thoroughly from my iniquity,
>   and cleanse me from my sin.

Had David not repented, perhaps the salt and light of the people of God would have been reduced to ashes and darkness.

The role of the church in our age must also be a prophetic voice to the powers that be so the effect of the light and salt of the kingdom is not reduced to ashes. The "Bathshebas" on the deck of the roof today are whatever is sought by those who give in to greed and lust for power. Whatever stands in the way of achieving power is crushed. There are good people in power who look out of their window and see "Bathsheba's" beauty. They cannot resist going to bed with her but never find it in their heart to repent when the evil deed is done. Like David, who had Bathsheba's husband killed, they will commit murder as a cover for their wrongdoings.

Revelation 17 describes the great harlot with whom the kings of the earth have committed fornication. The woman portrayed as the harlot has a golden cup in her hand. On her forehead is written "Babylon." Babylon is a world power corrupted through accumulating wealth. Its methods of getting rich may have been selfish use of its natural resources, taking away land from original occupants, exploiting weaker nations by its imperialistic tactics, increasing the possibility of global war by peddling its military hardware and training other nations to torture people.

Babylon is not sensitive to the needs of its own poor. Babylon refuses to convict those who bomb churches and kill little children. It creates a climate that sanctions the killing of those who call for social justice. It makes war on foreign soil and destroys weaker nations. Babylon takes away milk from hungry children to enlarge its military budget. Servants of Babylon misuse large sums of money intended for programs for the poor. Babylon cannot understand the teachings of Jesus in the Sermon on the Mount or Scriptural jubilee teachings.

Babylon does go to church. It is known to temper the tone of the preacher. It is not immune to making power plays to shape the church in Babylon's best interest. It makes the cross safe by couching it in the comfortable pew.

Babylon refuses to abide by its own laws while at the same time it cries law and order. Babylon has been effective in leading the church to withdraw from its concern for the powerless. Babylon feels good when the church follows Babylon's expertise and develops Babylon's value system for the church's program. Babylon uses biblical language to support its economic value system with the words, "In God We Trust." Babylon has prayer breakfasts and dumps napalm on innocent children.

How does Nathan approach modern Christians who are sleeping with the harlot? The church that cares about justice must cry out when Babylon uses the powerless as fodder to feed its own appetite for wealth and power. A church that is salt and light in the world can hear the voice of Paul: "Do not be conformed to this world, but be transformed by the renewing of your minds, so that you may discern what is the will of God - what is good and acceptable and perfect" (Rom. 12:2).

Rooted deeply in our history and theology is a biblical understanding of service and mission shaped by the Gospels and the experience and wisdom of the early church. The drawing of lines between evangelism and cup-of-cold-water ministries is a rather recent development. The first-century Christians expected the same quality of spiritual maturity from candidates for the role of deacon as they did for the role of bishop. Both needed to be equally filled with the Spirit of God. There were no descriptive designations that set one form of ministry above another. The deacons were appointed to care for the needy among them. But there are accounts of their preaching and teaching as well as serving tables.

To take lightly the history of the people of God throughout the generations is a formula for taking wrong turns along the road. Voluntary service is not an invention of the last half of the twentieth century. Since the beginning of the Anabaptist movement in the sixteenth century, there are stories recorded of how the faith of a people moved them to serve others. Participants in the Anabaptist movement (along, of course, with people of other faith traditions) gave their lives to serve people, including their enemies.

The voluntary service program in the Mennonite church did not start during World War II. It started in 1569, when Anabaptist Dirk Willems was fleeing across a frozen river. His pursuer broke through the ice. Dirk turned to rescue him, a kindness that cost Dirk his life. Perhaps Mennonite voluntary service started with Menno Simons' plea before the magistrate to deal justly and compassionately with the poor peasants. Maybe voluntary service began when Grebel, Blaurock, and Manz committed each other to mission and service during the first baptism among the Anabaptists, which helped found the movement. Anabaptism encompassed a cross-cultural grouping of farmers, peasants, city planners, and religious leaders, all uniting into one body of believers. Their different social backgrounds were all directed into a common cause: working out obedience to Jesus.

The beginning of the church's mission goes back to the teachings of Jesus. "Inasmuch as you have done it unto the least of these, you have done it unto me" is the New Testament formula. In fact the call to mission and service goes back to creation, when God gave the human family the mandate to care for creation.

Our common cause today is not to ask how we can build a political structure to do mission. Whenever we build a structure, we try to construct it so it will offend no one and still serve everyone. That is not to say that we don't need some organization to make best use of the gifts God has given to the church. Our common cause is to seek out what obedience to Jesus means for the twenty-first century.

A story is told about a small village that had a dangerous curve in the road at its entrance. In the most dangerous part of the curve was a huge bolder. Many accidents happened and lives were lost. The community called a meeting. Many ideas were placed on the table but the most attractive suggestion was to buy a new ambulance so injured victims could be transported to the hospital.

The community was proud when the shiny new vehicle arrived. People volunteered to keep the ambulance clean and shiny. Accidents continued to happen but more lives were saved. It wasn't long until people complained that the many accidents were causing too much wear on the ambulance. More time was spent on keeping the ambulance clean and less was spent on the victims. The ambulance was kept spic-and-span while the accidents continued to mount. The victims called a meeting to complain about the continuing lose of life. But the keepers of the ambulance could not see beyond caring for their shiny toy. All their energy went into maintaining the ambulance, when with a little energy and foresight the problem could have been solved by removing the bolder.

Sometimes the structures to do mission become more important than the mission. We care for the ambulance instead of removing the boulder. Sometimes the strategy we devise will not work. But since it was a good idea, we try to make the idea work while the injuries continue. The mission of the church is to identify the boulders in the road that cause destruction of lives.

While structures are needed to make best use of the gifts in the church, structures are not the final answer. I recall a story of our neighbor on the farm in Zurich, Ontario, where I grew up. He had a silo no longer used to store silage. The silo had only small holes where one could enter to fork out the feed. This farmer put a little calf into the silo to feed it and nurture it during the summer. Come fall the calf had grown so much he could not longer get it out through the small hole. We need to be careful we do not get ourselves locked into a silo of bureaucratic structures where we grow good ideas but cannot get them out of the holes. We can grow nice fat calves in the boardrooms of institutions, but the real test comes when we try to get them out of the hole.

A lot of energy has been consumed in recent decades, for example, to develop a church growth philosophy. Many precious trees have given their lives to be made into paper to publish the volumes of books on church growth. Some helpful material has been produced. Much of it, however, has involved putting the calf into the silo and not being able to get it out after it has grown. Philosophies of missions and service and of faith and practice that are trustworthy focus on justice.

The church should give witness to the state and shape its policies, but too often the state makes a path for the church to follow. When each federal election rolls around, I wonder what might be in that political cloud hanging low in the sky. I do not believe ultimate power lies in who is in government's high offices, but the power of such offices must be reckoned with. Embodied in high office are the hopes and dreams of oppressed people. When the powers that be fail to make good on their election promises, they increase the hopelessness and despair of the fringe people of society. It is then that the church must speak long and hard and stand firmly in the gap created through broken promises. While we are involved in worldly affairs we must avoid thinking like the world. The church must minister in the systems of the world but never develop a mentality comparable to that of the keepers of the system.

When the system fails, as it so often does, it is also in the church that forgiveness can be experiences. In 1963, during the heat of the civil rights movement, Sixteenth Street Baptist Church was bombed with fifteen sticks of dynamite. Two hundred people were in the church. Four girls were killed and twenty-four others injured. The Sunday school lesson in the girls' class that day was "The Love That Forgives." Finding within ourselves the ability to forgive those whose life is riddled with hate toward us is like a rainbow in the sky. It is a sign that God has chosen special people to preach the good news of peace. Peace, love, and justice are the brilliant colors of the rainbow.

Chapter 9

I Would Do It Over Again

I UNCOVERED IN MY FILE AN ARTICLE FROM *Sojourners* by Dom Helder Camara. In an address to Americans he said,

> I never tire of repeating that in all countries, in all races, in all religions, in all human groups, there exist small groups dedicated to the promotion of liberty and justice for all—and not only for the privileged individuals or countries. For all!
>
> Who made these groups to spring up throughout the world, in the North and South, in the West and in the East? Some individual? Some institution? Only the Spirit of God was able to make this happen.
>
> And the God of love, without a hint of hate, the God of the humble with only poor resources will use these weak instruments to raise up a union of the dispossessed from rich and poor countries. For there is an overwhelming hunger for justice as the supreme condition for peace.
>
> The God of the weak, of the small, of the poor, will work the marvel of making force give way to weakness. (*Sojourners*, July/August 1976)

I hope this book has made clear how many times in my ministry I discovered that God uses the weak, the powerless, the poor, and the nobodies to become somebodies and powerful forces for justice. I need to underscore again that my best teachers have been the gangs in the street, people in prison, victims of unjust systems, and those who have been forced to live on the margin. That does not mean that I do not value my teachers and leaders in college and seminary. But it is because of powerful lessons that my teachers in the street taught me that I would involve myself in justice ministries all over again. Of course I will not be able to do it over again, but I may have some time left to do better still than what I have done up to now.

As I reported earlier, the story in the Gospels of the four people taking the paralytic to the roof of the house where Jesus was teaching has special learning value for me. The house was full of Pharisees who wanted to hear and perhaps question Jesus. There was no room for the paralytic. Four courageous friends took the paralytic to the rooftop, opened the roof, and with ropes let the man down to Jesus.

I think I have been all of the actors in this drama. I know that at times I have been the Pharisee who kept people away from Jesus. Hopefully many more times I was one of the four men who carried the paralytic to the roof. I also have been the paralytic and experienced the joy of someone letting me down on ropes to be in the presence of Jesus.

It is risky to cut a hole in the roof to let someone get close to Jesus. One can only imagine what response there was from the Pharisees when the dust started falling around them, a gaping hole appeared above, and a man they likely considered unclean began to descend. Making holes in the roof creates dust and inconvenience for those in the room. You can be sure many of the bystanders were less then impressed with what was happening.

Cutting a hole in the roof is speaking out against evil that reduces the dignity of persons God created and loves. Cutting a hole in the roof of the house where the Pharisees sit almost guarantees a collision.

It is never a pleasant task to speak out against a system that can no longer do justice. Any system in the homestretch of its usefulness will withhold welcome to any one cutting a hole in its roof and letting down an unclean person. A system that is declining in power can welcome only that which will reinforce its present values. It has to contend for power to stay alive even when it knows it is not acting with compassion or truth. When the system injures people and the injured respond with anger, that anger is used by the system to justify its own action. If there is still a conscience left, it trains itself to believe wrong is right when it knows it is wrong.

I recall butchering days at home on the farm. People would gather early in the morning, then boil a large kettle of water to remove the hair from the hog. After the water was boiling and the butchering stage set, there was a procession to the barn to get the hogs. On butchering day, the hog was not about to voluntarily walk out of the barn, lie on its back, and patiently wait for the man with the knife to stick it into the pig's throat. It often took four men to wrestle the pig onto its back and hold it there until the blood gushed from its arteries.

Whenever injustice is done to a person or group of people, their struggle for survival is viewed as evil and as justifying the misdeeds of the powerful. The four strong men wrestling the pig to the ground is to me an image of a powerful institution no longer able to understand or tolerate justice. The innocent get rolled on their back and stuck with the knife. If the victim struggles, the system treats this as a sign that the system was right.

In the civil rights movement, some of the actions of the oppressed people were viewed by the powerful as inappropriate. The anger of the oppressed gave fodder to those who wanted to find ways to stand in the way of the movement. When women became empowered to protest being denied leadership roles in the church, the system began to panic. The pioneers in the movement often needed to overreact to get attention. Their overreaction was then viewed as inappropriate anger and as justifying the church's opposition to their pleas.

The issue of same-sex covenant relationships is now in the infancy stage of reaping the condemnation of the institution. The battle for truth concerning ordination for women was won by the early prophets in the system. Courageous women, with support of many men, laid their lives on the line and put truth and conscience ahead of political correctness. The civil rights movement made major strides because those who cared about justice could no longer remain silent. Both racial equality and encouraging women in ministry are still on long journeys. Perhaps the end will never come. The path for the church that welcomes same-sex persons in a covenant relationship is muddy and dangerous. The house is still full of Pharisees who will not let them come to Jesus.

Any system declining in power cannot afford to tolerate its critics even though they could be its best friend. Not to listen to the critics is to take a detour around truth. The Pharisees could not understand their chief critic, so they finally participated in a crucifixion.

Benjamin Hershey, a Mennonite preacher, once said that "We have dedicated ourselves to serve all men in every thing that can be helpful to the preservation of men's lives, but we find no freedom in giving, or doing, or assisting in anything by which men's lives are destroyed or hurt."

I would like to have a long chat with Ezekiel sometime. I would like to know what was the source of his visions and dreams. I would likely first ask him what he saw in the vision of the water gushing out of the temple. As the water from the temple flowed into the great sea, the stagnant sea water became fresh. I wonder if he might tell me that the temple represents all those who have voluntarily made commitments to become members of the kingdom of God. Because they are God's temple, the water that flows from them has the capacity to make the stagnant water fresh. I would then likely ask him to explain the significance for healing of the leaves. I wonder if he would say, "Look out into your community, open your eyes wide, and see the injustice that exists just around the corner. Use your leaves to bring healing to what is broken."

I would also like to chat with Nathan the prophet. Though he must have trembled, as I mentioned earlier, Nathan skillfully told David a story about a rich man who took the little pet lamb of a poor man to make a feast for an important guest. His anger kindled as he listened to the tear-jerking story, David's reply was that a man who did such an evil deed deserved punishment to the full extent of the law. Nathan looked David straight in the eye and said, "You are that man." Likewise whenever God's people see wrong they must speak out even if it is to the bishops, deacons, elders, conference moderators, and CEOs of the denomination. Included in the list of people whom prophets are called to engage about their responsibility for doing justice are political rulers. Presidents, prime ministers, and kings and princes are not excluded.

But seldom does the prophet speak out against those whom the powers have called "sinners." The support and confirmation of a community of such believers who care about justice is important to prophets. The judgment of a lone person may not always be the right one. To have a concern confirmed by more than one person gives it integrity and strength. I signed a letter one time for publication in a church paper asking the church to welcome persons of same-sex attraction into the church and bless the commitments they make with each other. I would never have written and signed a letter like that by myself. When more then six hundred respected and honorable people, committed to Christ and the church, signed it, that felt to me like it also carried the signature of God.

Had Nathan not been faithful in discharging his call from God, history might well have taken a much different twist. If David had not repented, there might have been no unfolding of salvation history. If prophets today are not faithful in calling into question sinful practices of discrimination and injustice, then soon the stories of salvation will be lost.

I don't think one can hear good news unless one *is* good news. Recently I eavesdropped on several gentlemen speaking the language I learned before I could speak English. At an auction sale, I listened to some Amish persons speaking Pennsylvania German as they conversed about the qualities of the animal about to hit the auction block. I was fascinated with the sounds, expressions, and rich meanings of some of the words. Some of the words really have no English translation. But the meanings of the words were still stored in my memory. I understood everything said; I suddenly was struck with the realization that I was one of them.

If we are not members of the kingdom, then it will be hard for us to understand the good news spoken by kingdom people. Kingdom people speak about justice. It is by being with others who also care about justice that we learn about justice. I am still trying to grow in my ability to communicate the good news by getting to know the "language" of those with whom I want to share it.

As I travel along the road of my ministry, I refresh myself by pondering for a while on the road of the past. I want to carry the peace and joy of the past with me to the end but unload the heavy, the painful, the mistakes and sins. I don't want to fall over them again nor do I want anyone else to stumble over them and injure themselves.

I look back and see how I enriched the life of a few people. I recall a conversation with a critic of mine who was chastising me for something I wrote which he interpreted as negative about church structures. After listening a while to his concern that I was a threat to the church, I replied that there are also some people who choose to stay in the church because someone has the courage to speak out when injustice is done.

I see some "fruit trees" I planted that are beginning to bear delicious fruit. I hear echoes that say "Thank you" for a helping hand. My files contain letters of gratitude for what I have written and said. My understanding that salvation has something to do with a change of mind and a movement toward a ministry of justice was appreciated by some inquiring minds. I know I plowed some fresh ground in urban ministry with few models to work from or strong mentors to guide me.

I know what it is like to be encouraged by some and criticized by others. Criticism can be turned into a special gift. Life brings us to many crossroads. Sometimes we make the wrong turns. Our critics become a gift to us in that they make us think more carefully before we choose which direction to go.

I know some people are convinced that any leadership I gave moved the church in a wrong direction. I received a letter from a person who said that since I like the communists so well, why don't I move to Russia. I took that as a compliment. If anyone during the 1960s was not called a communist, I suspect their ministry did not have a great deal of impact on the need for justice.

Another person whose life experiences were wrapped up in his small rural community informed me one time that I really did not know what the real issues of life are. As I reflected on that, I of course agreed with him. Every day was a day of new learning for me. Often I wished I could have stayed home on the farm in a conservative rural community where there seemed to be no need to ask hard questions. There always were more answers then questions.

I sensed that my concern over sins of racism, war, and discrimination against gays and lesbians was not always appreciated. I never could understand the fundamentalist view of Scripture. Fundamentalists could hold to a strong position on the inerrancy of the Bible but in the same breath deny the teachings of Jesus to love enemies.

Somewhere in my psyche or imagination I can hear some people suggest I have not understood the teachings of Jesus on riches. I certainly don't understand all of Jesus' teachings.

Since I discovered some saintly people whom I once would have regarded with suspicion, I have looked at wealth from a different perspective. By world standards, I am extremely wealthy. I have a bed to sleep on, a house for shelter, two cars in the garage, and enough food to eat. Jesus' hard sayings concerning wealth are meant for me as well as for anyone who has accumulated much larger quantities of wealth. Some say that the hard sayings of Jesus were not meant to be taken literally. The camel and the needle story was not meant to be taken literally. The eye of the needle was a hole in the wall around the city. Camels could get through by crawling on their knees after their master unloaded their cargo. Then the master could reach back and pull their load through. I think Jesus meant a literal needle where one could not pull the load through.

My suspicions of structures becoming more important then people were only appreciated by a few people. My salary for most of my earning years came from institutions and structures that had the potential for evil as well as good. When I suggested that structures are to serve the people, not people the structures, it seemed as though I was speaking heresy. But for some it was gospel.

If I could live my life over, I would likely do most of the same things again. I would certainly chose my same parents and the same community to nurture me. I would want to have my same brothers and sister as part of my family. I would want to go to the same church that nurtured my early years. I would want to grow up on the same farm I was raised on. I would want to trade in the same horses for a new John Deere tractor.

I would want to learn to drive a car with a Model-T Ford. I would certainly marry the same loving wife who was mother of my two children. I would want the same children again. I would want to marry the same loving wife again who entered my life after the mother of my children died. I would want to live in all the same places I lived and worked in ministry. I would want to work with the same people I once did. I would want to become a minister again. I would want to pastor the same congregations. I would want to be known as a person who cares about justice. If I were to do some more writing, it would be about justice.

The reality is that I cannot live my life again. I don't even have enough time left to correct all the mistakes I made along the way. The best I can do is ask for and accept God's forgiveness and make my last years as useful as I can.

Talking about mistakes, I don't think there are many left to make that I have not already made. But we may not bury ourselves in the mistakes of the past. To do so would rob us of the rich potential there is in ministering during our senior years. There is nothing we can do about past errors. In one sense they are on permanent record. In another sense they are erased by God's love and grace. God in his mercy removes our sin and errors so they will not hinder our continued preaching of the good news of the gospel.

I did not always understand the background and culture in which I was nourished and through which my life values were shaped. I would not want to go back to all of it, but it is all part of who I am. Those of us who do not grasp the richness of our own culture often rebel. There *were* times I tried to deny who I was. I did not trumpet the fact that my roots were in the Amish tradition. I did not always like who I was. But I have never found another culture richer then my own. That is not to say it is better then another. We each must value our own culture to be healthy. To value our culture is to receive freedom and appreciation to value the culture of others as equal to our own. Meanwhile not to drink deeply from another culture will almost guarantee not fully valuing the richness of our own. My involvement in multicultural ministries was a rich gift to me.

Jesus became a multicultural person. He ministered to Jews and Samaritans. He related to the outcasts of society. He made friends with the rich. He cared for his family. One of his last concerns had to do with long-term care for his mother. The most important person in Jesus' life was his mother. She understood God's purpose for him and he trusted her. Because of his trust in his mother, he was able to extend his family to include other people.

The picture of heaven described in the Bible is of a gathering of people from many lands, tribes, languages, all joining in one common purpose of praising God. Without crosscultural experiences on earth, heaven might be a scary place!

If I could do it over again I would certainly take advantage again of any opportunities for instruction and preparation for ministry. We really never get totally prepared. It takes us a whole lifetime to accept that we are always in a process of preparation.

I would also begin my ministry again in the inner city. I would begin there because so many good teachers are there. In the city gangs on the street understand the dynamics of a society that shuts people out. Extended families survive only because they have learned how to care for each other. Single parents have learned how to raise children with dignity. There is brokenness in cities that helps urban people develop a dependency on God. The veneer is removed so real people can emerge.

If I could live my life over again, I would be more careful how I use words. People do remember some things we say, good or bad. I met a saintly lady in the hall of a retirement center recently. She reminded me that some fifty years ago I visited at her home. I did not remember until she jogged my memory. In fact I do not recall having met her since that visit back in the late 1940s. She proceeded to tell me she still remembered something I said when I was there. It was a silly little joke.

I would likely accept again a churchwide assignment to work with social justice issues. I believe more strongly than ever that a congregation is a special gift from God to its community. I would accept an invitation again to lead a conference as missions minister charged with helping to develop new congregations. I would accept a call again to pastor a small struggling congregation. I would accept a call again from a conference to serve as an overseer for congregations.

It would be a harder choice to accept an invitation to work with a conference that would remove a congregation from membership because its members welcomed all those God brought to them. But I would again accept a invitation to walk with a congregation that has been removed from conference because it accepts all God's children.

At Souderton Mennonite Homes I sat recently with a ninety-three-year-old lady who inspired me. I inquired how she was doing. She promptly responded that she had slept so well the night before: "I had such a pleasant dream last night; I always have pleasant dreams." I sat wondering what in her life had brought her to the time when the curtain of life might soon fall and she continued to have pleasant dreams.

I could name a few reasons I would like to live another fifty years. I would like to spend another fifty years with my loving wife Mary. I know there likely will be music in heaven but none much sweeter then her voice.

Mary's gift of friendship is matched by none. She has a capacity to care about people that far exceeds any I have. When I am away overnight, sometimes I write her little messages and leave them under her pillow. I wrote this one time:

Days Away
A day away from you leaves an empty feeling
deep inside.
It says love is not measured by the mile
or by the yard.
It calls for memories to fill the gap
that longs for closeness
and thirsts deeply for your smile.

But I will not be long on this journey north.
I'll say hello to friends,
and give them a big hello from you,
then I will tell them
of your gracious spirit and your loving charm.
I will hold your grandchildren in my arms
like I know you would.

If I could sing, a tune would flow from
deep within my heart
and angels would bring flowers
in a two-horse cart.
So please have lots of fun.
Do things that bring you joy.

I'll pray for you when in my mind
I see that halo on your head
and wish that I could join you
in our cozy little bed.

Among the most joyous experiences for me is when we meet one of Mary's former students. Often the visitor is a mother with children the age the mother was when Mary had her in class. Frequently I hear, "You were the best teacher I ever had." Someone said recently that they hope Mary will still be teaching when a grandchild, now six, will be in her grade two class. I have always believed teachers will have a special reserved place in heaven. Since I married Mary, I have known that teachers will be in the head of the line when the awards are given out.

I would like to spent another fifty years with my children. I would like to watch my grandchildren grow up. Perhaps one will become prime minister of Canada. I would like to be there when when she or he gives the first speech to Parliament. I would sit in the front row carrying a banner, "That Is My Grandchild." Perhaps one will become a great scientist and find a permanent cure for the world's most deadly disease. Or maybe one will invent an energy source that will not injure the atmosphere and will provide safe fuel for every person's needs in the whole world. Maybe one will discover a new fresh way how God's will could "be done on earth as it is in heaven." My pride would reach its highest point if my grandchildren invested their lives to help a few people experience justice.

Even though our children are a ten-hour drive from us, they seem close. To experience love from one's children is a treasured gift. At Christmas time I write a little blessing for them. As part of our opening gifts tradition I like to read a few lines I wrote for them, such as these:

Blessing 2001
Another year has slipped away,
With rain and cold and heat and snow and our
Not knowing what tomorrow brings,
But love for family always grows.
Umberto and Johanna,
You're a special gift to all
To hear your little footsteps
and see you grow so tall.
You make us proud grandparents,
we love your hugs and smiles;
our love and blessing now be yours
and follow you through all the miles.

Michael and Diane,
Thank you for who you are;
your love feels so rich and pure,
like the sparkle of the brightest star.
And our love flows back to you,
words seem not enough to tell,
How cool refreshing love we have
like water from the deepest well.

Lorna and Roberto,
We hear music in our soul
when we drink deeply from your kindness,
as from a crafted crystal bowl.
Our love cannot be measured,
no cup is large enough
to hold the love within us.
You're a gift from God above.

If I could choose my family,
a family ready made,
I would search the ages
and cover every page.
And after all my searching,
I know there'd be none to find
like my very precious family—
So loving and so kind.

I wish I could say I was a perfect father. If any one can be perfect, their mother came the closest.

Life has measured out joy and sorrow for me. I look back and wonder at some decisions. At the moment they seemed right, but now, with a bit more history, it seems they could have been made more wisely. But I also look back and feel confident that many were the right decisions.

There were times I seriously doubted if the God I was taught about was really God. If there is a God, why is there so much suffering in the world? Why does God allow evil people to lead governments of the world? Why do churches that preach the gospel not live the gospel? Why are there hungry people in the world? Why does not everyone have a safe house to live in? I came to believe God asks those questions too. "Why don't my people care for my creation like I charged them to?"

While on a trip to New Zealand, I watched people do bungee jumping from a bridge into a deep canyon below. The people who jumped had a serious faith in the cord that kept them from injury. For me some of life has been bungee jumping. God always had a way to rekindle my faith. And in all my years that cord never failed me. That is the faith I will cling to for the rest of my journey. These few following lines are an effort to express my own feelings about faith.

When Faith

When faith takes exit out of one's life
And the reason for living takes wings,
There remains nothing firm or secure;
The bell of life no longer rings.

When faith is no longer a friend
And God moves much further away,
There is no longer a call within
To gather with friends to pray.

When trial and discouragement rise,
And faith is no longer at hand;
When tears stain the joys of the past,
And hope is built on the sand,
The memories of peace and content
Are like waves in the sea being tossed.
Fear like a rushing river roars,
And love is withered and lost.

But faith again like a mustard seed
Grows branches that reach into space.
And faith is rekindled by God's kindly touch
With a boundless measure of grace.

The Author

*H*UBERT SCHWARTZENTRUBER WAS BORN IN Zurich, Ontario, on a farm close to the shores of Lake Huron. His early years were spent on the farm. Later he attended Bible school and Bible institute in Kitchener, Ontario, for five years. He graduated from Eastern Mennonite College and also studied at Concordia Seminary and Webster College in St. Louis, Missouri.

Hubert has been a pastor for over forty years in a wide variety of settings, ranging from inner city congregations in St. Louis through rural congregations and now Souderton (Pa.) Mennonite Homes. He has also served as staff person in numerous denominational settings, including Mennonite Conference of Eastern Canada, Mennonite Board of Congregational Ministries (where he helped establish twenty congregations), and Franconia Conference.

Hubert and his wife, Mary Elizabeth Rittenhouse, are members of Plains Mennonite Church, Hatfield, Pennsylvania. They have two children and three grandchildren.